T0278293

IN THE SERVICE OF THE SHOGUN

IN THE
SERVICE
OF THE
SHOGUN
THE REAL STORY OF
WILLIAM ADAMS

FREDERIK CRYNS

REAKTION BOOKS

Published by
REAKTION BOOKS LTD
Unit 32, Waterside
44–48 Wharf Road
London NI 7UX, UK
www.reaktionbooks.co.uk

First published 2024
Copyright © Frederik Cryns 2024

The publishers would like to thank The Great Britain Sasakawa
Foundation for its support in the publication of this work

Printed and bound in Great Britain
by TJ Books Ltd, Padstow, Cornwall

A catalogue record for this book is available from the British Library

ISBN 978 1 78914 864 0

Contents

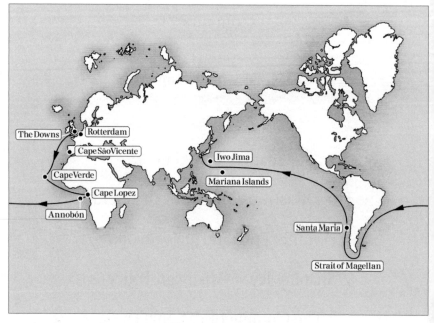

Voyage of the *Liefde*.

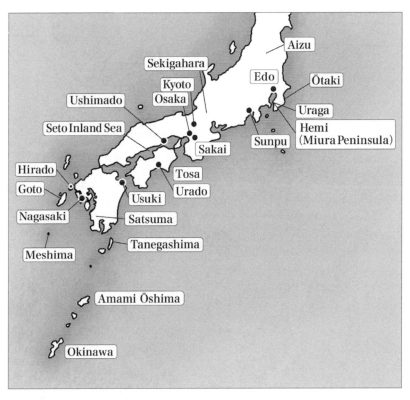

Japan in the 17th century.

East and Southeast Asia in the 17th century.

Note on Dates and Translations

There are Japanese, English, Dutch, Portuguese and Spanish sources related to Adams. In this book, I use dates as they appear in each one: the Japanese calendar in the Japanese sources, the Julian calendar in the English ones and the Gregorian calendar in the other sources.

All quotations have been changed to modern spelling except for those at the beginning of each chapter, where the original spelling has been retained. Place names are mostly given as they appear in the texts, but in modern spelling. For place names in Okinawa, I have used the Japanese names, per convention in modern research, which will hopefully aid any reader looking to source further information.

Preface

In the year 1600, an English pilot aboard a Dutch ship drifted ashore in Japan. His name was William Adams. He found himself in the midst of internal strife between various warlords. Soon, Adams gained the trust of the warlord Tokugawa Ieyasu. He became one of Ieyasu's close aides and had a significant influence on his foreign policy.

The story of an Englishman in the service of the shogun is something that captures the imagination. As a result, many books have been published about Adams's life. However, most of these books mix fact with fiction. Among others, James Clavell's novel *Shōgun* stands out. Adapted for film in 1980, and again in 2024 as an FX television series, *Shōgun* has attracted a large audience. In the novel, Adams is represented as John Blackthorne, an English sailor who washes ashore in medieval Japan. Like Adams, Blackthorne gains the trust of the most powerful feudal lord. In the novel, this is Lord Yoshii Toranaga, who, like Ieyasu, aspires to become shogun, the supreme military leader.

Although Clavell's novel is fiction, it is based on the author's meticulous study of Adams's life and of Japanese history. When I was given the opportunity to supervise the historical aspects of the FX television production, the thoroughness of Clavell's historical research often baffled me. I could recognize many aspects of the novel in the original sources. The lives and times of Adams, Ieyasu and Hosokawa Gracia (Lady Mariko in the novel) have been the main subject of my research at the university where I am currently a professor of Japanese history, the International Research Center for Japanese Studies (Nichibunken) in Kyoto.

In Clavell's novel, Blackthorne's life is full of adventure, and Adams's real life was by no means inferior to the novel in this respect. Clavell only used six months of Adams's life as a model for his novel, but the other 55 years are worth studying too.

We have many sources on Adams at our disposal. Several letters and journals written by Adams himself have survived. The diaries and letters relating to the English trading post at the small port town of Hirado, which operated in Japan from 1613 to 1623, also contain a wealth of accounts of Adams's activities. From these accounts, it is possible to reconstruct Adams's exploits faithfully.

So far, the study of Adams has been based mainly on the English sources, but the Dutch sources include a great deal of previously unknown information about Adams. The records of the Dutch trading post at Hirado, which was founded in 1609, contain many references to Adams. In addition, we have detailed records related to the voyage of the *Liefde*, the Dutch ship that brought Adams to Japan. These sources, combined with the few surviving Japanese, Portuguese and Spanish documents, allow us to get a clearer picture of Adams's life. They also shed light on the English and Dutch expansion into Asia, relations with the Portuguese and the Spanish, and Japan's foreign relations.

Adams's records reveal Ieyasu's diplomatic skills as well. Ieyasu had a keen interest in fostering good relations with other nations. This is not well known, perhaps because there are few Japanese sources on Ieyasu's diplomacy. For this reason, the Japanese often see him as the ruler who initiated Japan's policy of isolation. Yet, when we look at the Western sources, we find the opposite is true. Ieyasu sought to attract Westerners to Japan. Through the dialogues between Adams and Ieyasu, we discover examples of his brilliant political insights.

Although Adams's story was not as spectacular as Blackthorne's, it comes close in drama. Adams didn't live an ordinary life. He crossed the sea from England to far-off Japan, a daring feat in itself. The adventures during this voyage hold their own with a thrilling adventure story. Stranded in Japan, he was put in prison and feared for his life. Yet he overcame these misfortunes and gained the favour of the shogun. In this position, he exerted significant influence on Japan's relations with the Western world. But when Ieyasu died, Adams's fortunes took a dark turn. Hidetada, son of Ieyasu, took over, and Adams's influence became a thing of the past. In the end, Adams died in Hirado, far from the shogun's capital.

This book tells the authentic story of Adams's chequered life in the context of the times.

1

Adams's Early Life

I am a Kentish man, borne in the towen cauled Jellingham, 2 English myles from Rochester, 1 myle from Chattam wher the Kinge's shippes doe lye, and from the age of 12 yeares olde brought up in Lymehouse neere London, beinge apprentice 12 yeares to Mr Nico' Diggens, and myselfe have served for m'r and pilott in Hir Ma'tie's shippes, and about 11 or 12 yeares have served the Wor'll Company of Barbary Marchauntes until th'Indish traffick from Holland, w'ch Indish traffick I was desirous to make a littell experience of the small knowledg that God had geven mee.

WILLIAM ADAMS at Hirado to his 'unknown friends and countrymen', 23 October 1611

This quotation is from a letter written by Adams in 1611, after eleven years in Japan. He addressed the letter to any Englishman who might come across it and begins by introducing himself and writing briefly about his early life before sailing to Asia. Since we don't have any other sources about his early years, this is a particularly important document.

Knowing Adams's early life helps to contextualize his actions in Japan. To fully understand the significance of Adams's later role in Japan's foreign policy, we need to look at the environment in which he grew up. This was the Elizabethan era, an uncertain time marked by religious conflict and the constant threat of Spanish invasion.

Elizabethan England

William Adams was born in 1564 in the idyllic river port town of Gillingham, Kent, in the southeast of England. The baptismal register of St Mary Magdalene's Church reads: 'William Adams, son of John Adams baptized the 4 and 20th of September 1564.'

This was a very unstable time in England. The Protestant Queen Elizabeth had just ascended to the throne, and the Catholic powers in England threatened her rule. In 1569, five years after Adams's birth, the northern earls of England revolted, but the queen managed to put down the rebellion. At the same time, Pope Pius v issued a papal bull declaring Elizabeth a heretic and calling on the English people to overthrow her. Above all, Spain, the most powerful Catholic country in Europe, posed an enormous threat to the young queen.

Elizabeth's Protestant policies brought her into conflict with the Catholic King Philip II of Spain. Spain was one of the largest empires in the world. It had vast colonies, a strong economy and a powerful army. By contrast, Elizabethan England was a fragile country. Domestic religious conflict meant that Elizabeth's political base was unstable. Its economy was no match for Spain's: over-production of woollen cloth, England's main export, had led to a collapse in market prices. Most importantly, England's military power was nowhere near that of Spain, and repeated wars fought by Henry VIII, Elizabeth's father, had depleted the treasury.

For this reason, Elizabeth avoided all-out war with Spain for as long as possible. Before her reign, wars between European countries had mainly been the result of rivalries between monarchs. Once one side had won, the war was over, and the aftermath was settled with the transfer of land and ransoms. But religious wars, which became more frequent during the queen's reign, could only end with the complete destruction of the other side's faith. The English feared that France or Spain, the two greatest Catholic powers in Europe, would invade their country. To counter this threat, Elizabeth prepared for war by secretly buying arms and ammunition from the other Protestant countries.

With the publication of the Papal Bull, all English Catholics were suspected of aiding the Spanish in their invasion. Catholic officials throughout England who had not converted to Protestantism were considered a danger to the state. They were removed from their posts and replaced by loyal Protestants. It was against this background that anti-Catholic Puritanism was born. As a result, Protestantism and patriotism became linked to one another.

In 1571, when Adams was seven years old, a great conspiracy was uncovered. It involved the murder of Elizabeth and the accession to the English throne of Mary, the Catholic former queen of Scots. English Catholics, led by Thomas Howard, Duke of Norfolk, planned to rebel and prepare ships for the landing of Spanish troops. But the plot was foiled by a tip-off. The Duke of Norfolk was executed, and the Spanish ambassador was expelled from England. Anger against Spain was thus at its height, but Elizabeth continued to avoid formal war.

Meanwhile, at sea, the English began attacking Spanish ships. Spain had already imposed an embargo on English ships, and the merchants who had been trading in the Iberian countries were left with no way of doing business. They also had their ships and cargoes confiscated. In retaliation, the English seized Spanish vessels. Some of them even received permission from the queen to engage in privateering.

In the 1570s, while Adams was in his youth, the English made a series of expeditions to the Americas, plundering Spanish ships and bases. The most famous of these privateers was Francis Drake. Drake made several trips to the Caribbean in the 1560s with a fleet led by his cousin, John Hawkins. Initially, they bought slaves in Africa and sold them to settlers in the Spanish Caribbean colonies.

However, the king of Spain saw the invasion of his colonies by English ships as a violation of Spain's trade monopoly.

In 1568, an English fleet of five ships, including Drake's, was attacked by the Spanish fleet in the port of San Juan de Ulúa (now in the Mexican state of Veracruz). It was an act of treachery by the Spanish, for when the two fleets met a few days earlier, they had agreed to a truce. Three English ships were sunk in the surprise attack, and many English lives were lost. Only two of the smaller ships in the convoy escaped, one of which was Drake's. The two surviving vessels returned to England separately, both in shambles.

Of the hundreds of sailors on board, only seventy or eighty returned home. The news of the Spanish treachery and the cruel Inquisition carried out on the captives generated more resentment against Spain. The incident also had a profound effect on Drake's later life. Drake lost many of his relatives and friends in the battle. Determined to take his revenge, he embarked on a relentless campaign of plundering Spanish ships and bases. His aim was to inflict as much damage on the enemy as possible. This hatred of Spain was widespread in England during Adams's youth.

Drake's success gave the English people confidence that they could stand up to the Spanish Empire. However, Elizabeth refused to budge. To avoid an all-out war with Spain, she refrained from further escalation. It was enough for her to simply weaken the Spanish, and Drake's piracy was seen as a private enterprise in which the queen could enjoy plausible deniability. In contrast to Elizabeth's evasive strategy, many close to the queen wanted to confront the Spanish openly. They considered joining forces with the Protestant Dutch, who were in open rebellion against Spain, and alongside whom many English volunteers were already fighting.

After Portugal came under Philip's crown in 1580, the Spanish king gained an even more powerful maritime empire. The Spanish army captured one Dutch rebel stronghold after another, and the leader of the rebels, the Prince of Orange, was killed in 1584. Once the Spanish had crushed the rebellion, they could use the Low Countries (roughly modern-day Netherlands and Belgium) as a base for an invasion of England – after all, the Low Countries faced England across the Channel. In such a situation, the Spanish would be too close to England to be ignored.

Meanwhile, several Jesuits had travelled to England and were planning a revolt by Scottish and English Catholics to support the Spanish invasion. The plan was for an elite Spanish force to land in Scotland and march south with Scottish Catholics to overthrow Elizabeth. Mary, the imprisoned former queen of Scots, would then be installed on the English throne.

Fear of a Spanish invasion took over the lives of the English people. The danger came not only from abroad, but from the Catholic powers at home. People close to the queen thought that it would be better to resist Spain overseas. This would prevent the war from reaching English soil. Robert Dudley, the Earl of Leicester, had been pushing for war with Spain for some time. In 1585, he took his army to the Low Countries and joined the English volunteers who were already fighting on the side of the Dutch.

Dudley won some small victories at first, but lack of funds made it difficult to organize a proper army in the Netherlands. Casualties from battle and disease were high, and there were many deserters. On top of this, Welsh and Irish Catholics joined the Spanish army, which caused suspicion among the Dutch. The English suffered several defeats at the hands of the Spanish, and relations with the Dutch deteriorated. Dudley was forced to return to England without having achieved anything. Instead of weakening the Spanish threat, his expedition ended up strengthening it. Thus Adams spent his youth in a time of fear and uncertainty.

Growing Up

The town of Gillingham (now part of the unitary authority of Medway), where Adams was born, lies inland near the mouth of the River Medway, southeast of London. Gillingham had a thriving fishing industry and was a hub for the woollen trade with the Low Countries during the Middle Ages. In the sixteenth century, many merchants and craftsmen settled in the area. Nearby was the town of Chatham, known as the royal dockyard for Queen Elizabeth's fleet.

St Mary Magdalene's Church dominated the town. Its tower was visible for miles around and became a landmark for ships entering the Medway Estuary. The town to the west of the church expanded during the Middle Ages, and by the fourteenth century, a market was held there every Thursday. Yet in the sixteenth century, Gillingham was still a small town. The population is thought to have been around five hundred at the time of Adams's youth. There was only one street in the town, with houses on either side, and it was in one of these houses that Adams grew up. He lived there with his parents and siblings. According to the records of St Mary Magdalene's Church, he had a brother and a sister.

Compared to the north of England, the Kent area, including Gillingham, had a strong Anglican base. Each family prayed to God before every meal, and it was normal to attend services on Sundays and holidays. In sixteenth-century Europe, faith was a social norm that transcended the individual. Faith strengthened the bonds of the family and the community of each town. Letters of the period are therefore full of expressions of faith, and Adams's letters were no exception. For the English, the Reformation brought with it a sense of belonging to the English nation, alongside pride and self-confidence.

A notable characteristic of Adams was his literacy. Despite repeated attempts by the clergy to educate them, ordinary English people did not learn to write. Farmers, craftsmen and labourers did not need this skill to do their jobs. Among the common people, only merchants needed to be able to read and write in order to do business. Literacy was therefore seen by the public as one of the professional skills of merchants, apart from the upper classes and priests.

Because writing was not widely used as a means of communication among the general population, the acquisition of this skill required strong motivation on the part of students and their parents. Adams's parents seem to have had such motivation, and its efficacy is evident from the many letters that Adams wrote.

Apart from the baptismal records, there are no other references to Adams's parents, so we do not know what social status his father had. Nevertheless, it is clear that they were keen for their son to learn to read and write. This suggests that his father may have been a merchant, but nothing can be said for certain.

Literacy played a crucial role in social status. Those who could read and write had access to a wide range of knowledge. This allowed them to expand their activities in commerce, politics and other fields. Adams belonged to that class. Therefore, he could hope for some kind of career in the upper echelons of society.

At the age of twelve, Adams left his birthplace and went to Limehouse, a town near London on the banks of the River Thames. There he lived with Nicholas Diggins, a famous shipbuilder. Research by Richard Irving reveals that although Diggins owned a shipyard, he was not a shipwright but a navigator. Irving therefore concludes that Adams acquired his navigational skills during his apprenticeship.

Adams lived in Diggins's house as an apprentice. In those days, there was no clear line between work and home for a craftsman. In addition to the master and his family, several apprentices lived with him in this house. The relationship between master and apprentice did not stop at the professional level: the apprentice became a member of the master's family. The master played a role similar to that of a parent and was a source of emotional support. When Adams introduced himself in the letter from Japan to his 'unknown friends and countrymen', he made no mention of his father, but proudly wrote that he had been 'brought up in Lymehouse near London, being apprentice 12 years to Mr Nico' Diggens'.

Limehouse was a thriving outer port of London. Shipbuilding was booming, and the expansion of the industry supported the exploits of Drake and other privateers in the second half of the sixteenth century. Before that, shipbuilders did not have a high status. There were few of them in the Middle Ages, and the guilds were weak. But when Adams was a young man, the building of ships for the English merchant marine and the queen's fleet was flourishing. Demand for shipbuilders rose sharply, making it a popular occupation for young men of the lower classes.

Although Adams followed his apprenticeship as a navigator of ships, it is likely that he gained some knowledge of the craft of shipbuilding, owing to his master's shipyard. At the age of 24, after twelve long years of apprenticeship, Adams had perfected the art of navigation and joined the queen's fleet.

War

The queen's fleet should not be seen as a military organization managed in the way we know it today. It was not a permanent entity: when needed, a fleet was formed ad hoc by adding merchant ships to a small force of warships under the direct command of the queen.

These merchant ships were as battle-ready as warships. If they encountered pirates or enemy warships, they had to defend themselves. English merchants also often engaged in privateering, so in the event of war, their ships would be integrated into the queen's fleet. When Adams joined in 1588, the assembled fleet consisted of

226 ships, 192 of which were merchantmen that joined the fleet as the Spanish Armada sailed for England that year.

During Adams's apprenticeship at Limehouse, tensions between Spain and England reached their peak. In 1585, the Earl of Leicester arrived in the Low Countries to help the Dutch in their war against Spain. At the same time, Drake's fleet crossed the Atlantic to plunder Spanish strongholds in the Caribbean, such as Santo Domingo and Cartagena. These acts enraged Philip II. Until then, the Spanish king had been trying to bring down Elizabeth's reign from within. But Drake's attacks exposed weakness in the defences of Spain's vast colonies. To counter the threat of these attacks, Philip decided to invade England directly. To this end, he set about assembling a vast fleet.

In 1587, news of a planned invasion reached the English. Elizabeth ordered Drake to disrupt the building of the Spanish fleet. Drake soon sailed to Spain with a fleet of twenty ships. When he reached the Spanish coast, he met two Dutch vessels. The Dutchmen on board told him that many Spanish ships were anchored in Cádiz, a port in the southwest of Spain. This was the information Drake needed. He rushed to Cádiz, where he surprised the Spanish and destroyed their ships one by one. This daring attack delayed the completion of the Spanish fleet for almost a year.

Elizabeth used this precious time to prepare her defence. She began a campaign of imprisoning England's leading Catholics and executing Catholic missionaries who had infiltrated the country. She also organized militias and built a large fleet to intercept the Spanish Armada. Every port was ordered to provide ships and men. Such orders also reached Limehouse. No doubt that is what inspired Adams to join the queen's fleet.

Besides ships and men, the fleet also needed competent captains, and Adams qualified for the task, having just finished his apprenticeship. He may have been chosen by an acquaintance of Diggins, who, as a renowned shipbuilder, had a wide network of contacts. The Harleian Collection of Manuscripts in the British Library holds a list of ships that took part in the battle against the Spanish Armada. The *Richard Duffylde*, with 'William Adams' as its captain and a crew of 25 men, is listed as one of the fifteen ships that carried provisions westwards to Plymouth.

Drake's fleet had been anchored in Plymouth since March 1588 to defend the west coast of England. In May, however, Lord High Admiral Charles Howard also moved most of his fleet to Plymouth. The original strategy was to divide the navy into three units, and each unit would be responsible for defending an assigned zone. Apart from Drake's fleet in the west, Howard would command the main fleet at Dover, while Henry Seymour would prevent the Spanish army from embarking in occupied Flanders. But the Council of War changed this strategy at Drake's request to attack the Spanish Armada in Spain itself. The arrival of the main fleet posed a major problem, since Plymouth did not have enough food for so many sailors. On 22 June, fifteen ships sent from London arrived in Plymouth with a month's supply of provisions. Adams's ship was one of them.

With the problem of food shortages likely to recur in due course, Howard ordered an immediate departure for Spain. The English attempted to sail three times in May and June, but on all three occasions they were driven back to port by headwinds. While the queen's fleet was busy challenging the winds, the Spanish fleet suddenly arrived off the English coast on 19 July. The sight of the mighty Armada must have been terrifying to the young Adams. The Spanish ships were huge compared to the English ones.

The English sailed in great haste and attacked. Because of their size, the English ships were much more manoeuvrable than those of the Spanish. However, they couldn't compete in close combat, so they took care to keep their distance. To prevent the Spanish from firing back, they would discharge from afar, then retreat further still to reload their cannon. The Spanish were

Jan Luyken, *Downfall of the Spanish Armada*, 1730, etching.

unable to respond but suffered little damage. This stalemate lasted for some time.

The English repeatedly ran out of ammunition and had to retreat and reload from supply ships. Whether Adams resupplied the fleet from the rear or took part in the battle himself is not clear. Irving makes a strong case for the latter, but no sources survive to verify this hypothesis.

Undeterred by the English attack, the Spanish fleet sailed on and anchored off Calais in France. There they waited for the main army, which was supposed to join them from Flanders by means of transport ships. But the Dutch fleet blocked their way. The Spanish fleet, now idle off the coast of Calais, became an easy target, and the English did not waste the opportunity. At midnight on 28 July, they sent eight fire ships towards their enemies.

These fire ships caused a great panic. By dawn, the Spanish ships were scattered across the sea, prey to English cannon. Struggling to regain cohesion, the Spanish fleet fled north, attempting to return to Spain around the west coast of Ireland. But many Spanish ships, damaged by the English pounding, were wrecked on the Irish coast. Only a few managed to escape.

The news of this resounding victory brought joy to the hearts of the English people. Protestant churches across the country held special services to give thanks to God. But the victory came at a high cost. With severe shortages, the sailors fought without enough food to last ten days at sea. More than 8,000 men died of hunger and disease. Being in charge of supply, the situation must have been distressing for Adams.

After the victory over the Spanish, the queen's fleet was disbanded, and the sailors were dismissed. Suddenly unemployed, Adams had to find other work.

The Company of Barbary Merchants

Having lost his position in the queen's fleet, Adams next went to work for the 'Wor'll Company of Barbary Marchauntes'. This company, which we will refer to as the 'Barbary Company', had a monopoly on the trade between England and Morocco. The name 'Barbary' refers to the region on the north coast of Africa inhabited by Berbers.

Adams doesn't disclose how he served the company in his writings, but given his background, he probably sailed on the company's ships as a captain or a pilot. Having achieved some stability in his life, he married Mary Hyn on 20 August 1589, in the parish church of St Dunstan in Stepney. By this marriage he had a son and a daughter. Nothing is known of the son, but the daughter, named Deliverance, is mentioned in the documents of the English East India Company. Her name referred to the fact that God had saved England from the Spanish invasion, suggesting that the defeat of the Armada meant a lot to Adams. She married Ralph Goodchild, a sailor, at St Dunstan's Church on 30 September 1618.

That Adams married in Stepney suggests he settled there or in nearby Limehouse. Close to London on the north bank of the Thames, Stepney had a thriving shipbuilding industry. While Limehouse built large ships, Stepney specialized mainly in smaller vessels. Like Adams, many who had been discharged from the queen's fleet settled there, and by the late sixteenth century, the area was crowded with sailors.

Above the west entrance to St Dunstan's Church is a sculpture of a ship. This testifies to the close connection between this place and seafarers. In fact, St Dunstan's was known as the 'Church of the High Seas'. All seamen were considered parishioners of the

West entrance to the tower of St Dunstan's Church, Stepney, London, with a sculpture of a ship on the left-hand side above the door.

church. Adams's decision to live in this area may have been based on his longing for the sea. As a servant of the Barbary Company, he probably spent most of his time at sea, away from his family. This must have caused Mary and her children considerable anxiety.

Life at sea was fraught with danger. In those days, ships were made of wood, and the slightest neglect of repairs increased the likelihood of shipwreck. Sea battles were common in the event of an encounter with enemy vessels or pirate ships, and even if sailors did not die as a result of the violence, they could be taken prisoner or sold into slavery. Fresh food was not available on board, and as a result, malnutrition was common, which led to the spread of scurvy among the sailors. Moreover, the ships were overcrowded, so when an epidemic broke out, it spread quickly. Every time Adams went to sea, his family must have feared that he would never return.

Adams worked for the Barbary Company for just under ten years. He was in the prime of life, between the ages of 25 and 33. We can assume that he made several voyages to Morocco. Morocco was surrounded by the mighty countries of Turkey, Spain and Portugal. Turkey's influence extended as far as Algeria, to the east of Morocco. The transit trade port of Melilla, to the northeast of Morocco, had become a Spanish enclave. In addition, parts of Morocco were under Portuguese rule. But by the middle of the sixteenth century, Sultan Ahmad Mansur Zahabi resisted the Portuguese and regained part of his country from them.

Trade between England and Morocco began in the 1550s. The first voyages were made on an irregular basis. Early on, however, there was a shift to organized trade with Morocco for strategic reasons, since England needed nitre for its gunpowder stockpiles in the war against Spain. The prospect of obtaining this vital mineral in Morocco led to an emphasis on trade with the country. One man involved in the arms trade with the Moroccan king was Robert Dudley, the first Earl of Leicester and a close adviser to Queen Elizabeth. We have seen above that Dudley led the English reinforcements against the Spanish in the Netherlands. In order to control the import of raw materials for ammunition, and also to finance the war effort, he thought it necessary to set up a company with a monopoly on the Moroccan trade.

In this context, on 5 July 1585, Queen Elizabeth granted Dudley, his brother Ambrose Dudley, Earl of Warwick, and forty London merchants a patent to trade with Morocco. Dudley then formed the Barbary Company. Trading activities were not conducted as a single entity: each of the company's members, the London merchants, sent their own ships to trade. Adams seems to have been employed by one of these merchants as a captain or pilot, but even as captain, he would not have had the highest position on the ship – the merchants made the decisions on board, and the captain advised them on matters of navigation.

What can be said about the merchants involved in the Barbary trade is that their businesses varied in size and the products they traded were diverse. The ships sent by Dudley himself exported metals such as iron, lead and tin and imported nitre. The goods carried on the ships of the London merchants consisted mainly of woollen cloth, which was traded for sugar. There are few sources for the trading activities of the members. From the few that do exist, however, we can deduce that trade with Morocco itself did not live up to the merchants' expectations. The volume of trade was small, and customs duties, gifts to the king and his officials and various local expenses seem to have brought them little profit.

So why did they continue to trade? They kept sending ships because, as well as commerce, these merchants also engaged in privateering. To sail to Morocco, they had to cross the main Spanish and Portuguese shipping lanes, and these lanes were full of enemy ships, ready to be captured. The route to Morocco therefore provided a favourable environment for privateers. When a ship sailed from England to Morocco, its mission always consisted of a combination of trade and plunder. Usually, before or after trading in

Morocco, the ships would spend several months cruising the waters around the Iberian Peninsula in search of enemies.

To ensure a successful capture, the company's ships were heavily armed and carried larger crews than usual. The extra manpower was needed to board the enemy ships. Because of their routes in hostile waters, the Barbary Company became much more militant than its contemporaries who sailed to other parts of the world, such as Germany or Russia. When the ships returned to London, they often brought back captured ships.

Take, for example, the story of the *Amity*, a Barbary merchantman. In 1592, on his way back to England from Morocco, the ship's captain, Thomas White, spotted two large Spanish ships. The crew of the *Amity* boarded the Spanish ships and after a fierce battle, the Spanish surrendered. Captain White took the two captured ships back to London. It must have been quite a sight to see the *Amity*, a ship of only 100 tonnes, dragging two large Spanish ships of several hundred tonnes into the Thames. The crew made a lot of money because, as was customary, they received a share of the captured cargo.

This type of privateering was fraught with danger. Capturing a prize meant boarding the enemy ship, and many of the crew could lose their lives in the close combat that followed. Besides, they were in danger of being captured themselves. For example, in 1591, five Spanish warships attacked the *Dolphin*, a Barbary merchantman, in the Strait of Gibraltar. She put up a brave fight, but her powder magazine exploded; she sank, and all the men on board drowned. As few sources exist on the Barbary Company, Adams's exploits during his service are unknown. However, given the nature of the Barbary trade, it is likely that Adams gained a great deal of combat experience.

The dissolution of the Barbary Company in 1597 coincided with the start of a series of Dutch fleets sailing to Asia. Since trade with Morocco moved forward on a private basis, Adams could have continued as a captain or pilot on board an independent merchantman, but his mind was elsewhere. He wanted to apply the navigational skills he had developed to the uncharted waters of Asia.

English Expansion in Asia

Before 1580, the English knew little about East Asia. Only the Spanish and Portuguese had sailed to Asian waters, and in order to maintain their trade monopoly, they kept information about the geography, routes and political situation of the Asian countries secret. However, in the middle of the sixteenth century, the Jesuits began to travel to Asia on Portuguese ships. Unlike the traders, they wanted the Christian community to know about their work in the region, and took to publishing reports on their activities and the political events in Asian countries. Some of the Jesuits' books found their way into the hands of English readers. It was through such works that Adams learned about Japan.

In 1580, Drake's exploits gave the English their first direct information from Asia. Always looking for new ways to attack the Spanish, Drake set sail for South America in 1577 with a fleet of five ships. He sailed through the Strait of Magellan and attacked the Spanish strongholds and ships on the west coast. Long before that, the Spanish had given up trying to sail through the Strait. There were many obstacles to using this route, including hostilities from the natives, strong winds and currents and severe cold. As a solution to these problems, the Spanish conducted all traffic between the Atlantic and Pacific overland through Mexico. They didn't expect the English to use the Strait of Magellan. Hence, they left their bases on the west coast unprotected. Drake attacked these vulnerable strongholds one by one and captured two Spanish ships full of treasure.

Due to storms and other factors, only the flagship *Golden Hind* survived. Drake took the vessel north, filled with gold and silver. When he reached northern California, he landed and repaired the ship. Fully prepared, he then crossed the Pacific and reached the Moluccas. This was the first time an English ship had entered Asian waters. After purchasing spices, Drake returned to England via the Cape of Good Hope in September 1580.

Crossing the Pacific was not part of the original plan: Drake intended to raid Spanish bases in South America and return to England by the same route he had come. The reason for the sudden change is unknown – perhaps Drake thought it too risky for a single ship full of treasure to sail once more through the Strait of Magellan – but a small English ship circumnavigating the globe was unprecedented.

With this achievement, Asia suddenly came into sight of the English. It gave them confidence that they could go anywhere in the world, whereas before, English ships had only sailed as far as the Caribbean. On his return, Drake became a national hero and was knighted. The *Golden Hind* was permanently docked at Deptford on the south bank of the Thames, just outside London, and soon became a tourist attraction.

Hoping to repeat Drake's feat, an adventurer called Thomas Cavendish set sail from Plymouth in 1586 with a fleet of three ships. Like Drake, he passed through the Strait of Magellan and attacked Spanish strongholds in South America. Off the coast of California, he captured a Spanish ship, the *Santa Ana*, which had come from Asia and was loaded with treasure.

Cavendish then followed in Drake's footsteps, crossing the Pacific and arriving in the Philippines. After attacking the Spanish bases there, he returned to England via the Cape of Good Hope. Cavendish arrived in Plymouth in September 1588, six weeks after the English fleet had defeated the Spanish Armada, and the whole of England was rejoicing. Cavendish was welcomed with open arms by Queen Elizabeth, and, like Drake, was knighted.

When he plundered the treasure of the *Santa Ana*, Cavendish transferred some of its crew to his own ship. Among them were two Japanese boys. The eldest, about twenty years old, was called Christopher; the other Cosmus, about seventeen. As their Western names would suggest, these two had converted to Catholicism. Both could read and write Japanese, which meant they belonged to the upper classes. As they had sailed from the Philippines to Mexico, it is likely that they also spoke Spanish and/or Portuguese. Cavendish wanted to use them as a source of information about Japan and the Philippines.

The two boys eventually settled in England. There are few records of their activities there, but we do know that they adapted to the English climate and that they spoke English well. The voyage from the Californian coast to England took almost a year, so they must have had plenty of time to learn and master English on board. The pair seem to have got on well with the English crew. It is likely that Adams had heard about them because his friend Timothy Shotten was part of the crew on Cavendish's circumnavigation.

Having tasted success, Cavendish organized a new fleet of five ships for another circumnavigation, setting sail from Plymouth in August 1591. This voyage, however, ended in disaster. Cavendish, and probably the two Japanese boys who had joined the expedition, died in the Atlantic. Few of his crew returned to England.

Behind the glory of the expeditions lay great sacrifice. Of the five ships that sailed in Drake's fleet, only one made it back to England, and on Cavendish's first voyage, only one of the three ships returned home. Two-thirds of each crew would die owing to starvation, disease or fighting. In these circumstances, sailing around the world was a real feat, and not an easy one. The English attempted several more expeditions to Asia, but none were successful. These ventures required large amounts of money and involved a great deal of risk, and by the 1590s, no English merchant wanted to take such a chance. They concentrated on privateering in the Caribbean, which was easier to navigate and closer to home.

Nevertheless, inspired by the success of Drake and Cavendish, many English sailors dreamed of sailing to new waters. It was the Dutch who gave them the opportunity to make those dreams come true. In 1595, a fleet of four Dutch ships under Cornelis de Houtman set sail for Asia on a route around the Cape of Good Hope. A year later, they reached Bantam in Java but lost much of the crew and a ship along the way. The voyage proved unprofitable, but the return of Houtman's remaining ships to the Netherlands in 1597 showed that the Dutch could bypass the Portuguese and sail directly to Asia.

After Houtman's return, wealthy merchants began to set up trading companies in various ports around the country. In 1598 alone, five companies each sent a fleet of ships to Asia. The Dutch relied on their shipbuilding skills, abundant capital, trading skills and information-gathering abilities to make the most of their ventures in Asia.

For English sailors, the chance to sail to Asia on Dutch ships looked attractive. The English and the Dutch had been friends in the war against Spain. There was also cooperation in seafaring. Dutch crews served in Drake's and Cavendish's fleets. Conversely, experienced English sailors were recruited to serve on Dutch ships. As they sought to expand into Asia, the Dutch could certainly use someone like Adams, with his long experience of navigation.

2

The Disastrous Voyage of the *Liefde*

Soe, in the yeare of our Lord 1598, I was hired for Pilott-Major of the fleet of 5 saile w'ch was made ready by th'Indish Company, Poeter vander Hag and Haunce vander Veeke. The Gennerall of this fleet was a marchaunt cauled Jaques Maihore, in w'ch shipp, being Admirall, I was pilott of.

WILLIAM ADAMS at Hirado to his 'unknown friends and countrymen', 23 October 1611

As Adams wrote in the letter to his 'unknown friends and countrymen', the opportunity to travel to Asia presented itself when Adams heard of the imminent dispatch of a fleet of five ships organized in Rotterdam. The project was initiated by a merchant called Pieter van der Haegen, who kept the true purpose of the fleet a secret. It would take Adams almost two years of unprecedented calamity and hardship before he reached Japan.

Rotterdam

Pieter van der Haegen conducted business in Amsterdam and Rotterdam and traded with various parts of Europe. On one occasion he even sent a fleet to America. Although the Netherlands were at war with the Iberian countries, Van der Haegen also traded successfully with Portugal's African strongholds. He was a native of Antwerp, which became the centre of the independence movement during the war against Spain. However, after a year of fierce fighting, the city surrendered to Spanish troops in 1585. After that, Antwerp, along with the cities of the southern Netherlands, remained under Spanish rule, and only the northern Netherlands gained independence from Spain. This new state called itself the United Provinces.

Before the war, Antwerp was one of the most prosperous cities in Europe. With close links to the Iberian countries, it was the centre of trade and finance in northwestern Europe. The city was badly damaged during the war. As a result, many wealthy Antwerp merchants moved to Amsterdam and Rotterdam in the United Provinces. These merchants brought their wealth and networks with them to the Netherlands, where they began active trading careers. Van der Haegen was one of them.

Shortly after Houtman's ship returned from Asia in August 1597, Van der Haegen began planning to send a fleet to Asia. To this end, he called on some of his friends. A wealthy banker called Johan van der Veken, who, like Van der Haegen, was from Antwerp and had settled in Rotterdam, agreed to set up a joint venture.

Several other merchants also joined the project. The involvement of Hans Broers is noteworthy. He was an Amsterdam merchant who had founded the Dutch Barbary Company in 1592 with Sebald de Weert, a merchant from Antwerp. De Weert may have been the point of contact between Adams and the project.

The Dutch Barbary Company, like the English Barbary Company, traded with Morocco. Apart from Sebald de Weert, who went to Morocco himself, at least one of De Weert's brothers, David de Weert, is known to have stayed there for some time. When Dutch and English ships arrived, it was not unusual for them to stay there for months. This was because trade negotiations and the unloading of goods usually took a long time.

When Adams sailed to Morocco for the English Barbary Company, he had little to do while the ship was at anchor. During that time, Adams simply waited for the merchants to finish their business. The Dutch, his fellow Protestants and comrades-in-arms, were also there. It would have been natural for them to get to know each other. In this environment, Adams would have had ample opportunity to discuss many things with the De Weert brothers. It was during these conversations that he would have learned of their plans to travel to Asia.

Adams arrived in the United Provinces in the spring of 1598. He probably spent some time in Rotterdam before the ships sailed. Situated on the Meuse River, which flows into the North Sea, Rotterdam had a thriving economy. In the second half of the sixteenth century, wealthy merchants from Antwerp fled the war and settled in the city. Its population exploded, reaching over

William Adams says goodbye to his wife and children, illustration from William Dalton, *Will Adams, the First Englishman in Japan* (1866).

10,000 by the end of the century, making it one of the largest cities in Europe.

The people of Rotterdam have always been religiously tolerant: while the wars raged, the city remained on the sidelines. In this environment, merchants from Antwerp were able to operate freely, and Rotterdam quickly grew into an international trading port. Several broad canals crossed the city, which was surrounded by a wide water moat and walls, and countless large ships moored in the canals and docks. In the centre of the city stood the magnificent town hall, with a large church nearby. The markets were full of people, and sailors came from all over the United Provinces to join the Van der Haegen fleet. Foreigners also joined them: according to various accounts, there were eight or ten French soldiers and dozens of Englishmen on board. Even a Portuguese boy is mentioned in the records.

The total number of sailors in the fleet amounted to about five hundred. At the same time, a Rotterdam innkeeper called Olivier van Noort was preparing to leave for Asia with four ships. About four hundred sailors joined his fleet. In total, a staggering nine hundred sailors stayed in Rotterdam. For a city of 10,000 inhabitants, this was a considerable number.

Adams did not arrive in Rotterdam alone. His brother Thomas was with him, as were his good friends Timothy Shotten and Thomas Spring, both English pilots. It is likely that they travelled to Rotterdam together. Where would they have stayed in a city full of sailors waiting to sail on the two fleets? The ordinary sailors would have already been on board, but we don't know if this was the case for Adams and the others. Because of their position as pilots, they might have stayed at an inn.

Shotten had been to Asia before. He was part of the crew of Cavendish's fleet that had circumnavigated the globe. While waiting to depart, Adams had plenty of time to hear about Shotten's experiences in Asia. From what the group heard, they must have been eager to see these little-known lands for themselves.

Van der Haegen fleet, *c.* 1600, etching from F. C. Wieder,
De reis van Mahu en de Cordes (1923).

While Adams and his men waited, the five ships that Van der Haegen had purchased were fitted out. We have detailed information about their appearance from Spanish records, since at a later date, the Spanish would capture and interrogate some of the crew. These records are still kept in the Archivo General de Indias in Seville. Of the five ships, the *Hoop* (pronounced 'hope'), a 500-tonne galleon, was the largest and therefore the flagship. It had three masts and an image of a woman on its stern. It carried 130 men and was armed with 34 guns. Adams, Shotten and Spring were assigned to this ship. Its captain was Jacques Mahu, the admiral of the fleet.

Mahu was from Cologne, Germany. A relative of Van der Haegen's lived in Cologne, and it may have been through this connection that he was chosen as admiral. Mahu was 34 when the fleet set sail, the same age as Adams. He is described in the records as a courteous and mild-mannered man. Emanuel van Meteren, consul of the Dutch merchants in London, calls him 'an experienced and able merchant'. Yet this was the first time he had been given the heavy responsibility of admiral of a fleet. He was chosen not for his qualities as a sailor or a leader, but for his connections with other merchants. This made him somewhat unreliable to lead a fleet of five ships. Having a merchant who knew little about the sea in charge must have been a source of concern for Adams.

Adams's brother Thomas was assigned to the sub-flagship, the *Liefde* (Charity). The 300-tonne, two-masted *Liefde* carried a crew of 110 men and eighteen guns, and a small collapsible pinnace was stored on board. The ship was originally named *Erasmus*: on the stern stood a statue of the Rotterdam scholar. Desiderius Erasmus, a Catholic priest and humanist, lived in the second half of the fifteenth century and the first half of the sixteenth century. His writings had a profound influence on both Catholics and Protestants. Although he didn't perform any heroic deeds, the people of Rotterdam were so proud of him that they called their city 'the city of Erasmus'.

Erasmus travelled extensively in Europe. He spent a few years in England, and the English still call him 'Erasmus of Cambridge'. Adams must have felt a certain kinship with the scholar. During his stay in Rotterdam, he may have visited Erasmus' birthplace, which was already a museum at the time. At the very least, he would have seen the wooden statue of Erasmus in the central square. A humanist at heart, Erasmus was a true symbol of Rotterdam. No wonder his statue was displayed on one of the ships that left the city. Incidentally, this statue is the only surviving part of the ship and is kept in the Tokyo National Museum.

Simon de Cordes became captain of the *Liefde* and second in command of the fleet. De Cordes was a wealthy Antwerp merchant. He had lived in Lisbon for many years to conduct his business, but moved to Amsterdam in the early 1590s. Forty years old at the time of the fleet's departure, he was probably an acquaintance of Van der Haegen or Van der Veken and helped to finance the fleet. Also on board the *Liefde* was Simon de Cordes's son of the same name, a young man of about eighteen.

The third ship, the *Geloof* (Faith), was a two-masted ship of 320 tonnes, similar in size to the *Liefde*. She had a crew of 109 men and twenty cannons. The Ten Commandments could be seen on the stern hull, with a picture of a woman next to it. The captain of the ship was a 38-year-old man named Gerrit van Beuningen, a German-born Amsterdam merchant and a troublesome character. As a merchant officer, he was on board the aforementioned Houtman's fleet, but his arbitrary behaviour during the voyage was quite severe. To maintain order, Houtman kept him in irons for most of the voyage.

Despite this, Van der Haegen and his colleagues appointed Van Beuningen as one of their captains: from the descriptions of his behaviour in Houtman's diary, it seems that he had a talent for presenting himself as a capable leader. Whether this pretence was backed up by actual action, however, is dubious.

The *Trouw* (Loyalty), at 220 tonnes, was a little smaller than the *Liefde* and the *Geloof*. It had a crew of 86 men and sixteen guns. On the stern hull there was a painting of two hands facing each other. Jeurian van Bockholt, a 28-year-old from Dordrecht, commanded the ship. He suffered from weak health.

The fifth ship to join the fleet was the *Blijde Boodschap* (Good Tidings), standing at 150 tonnes. The other ships were quite large vessels, whereas this ship was a yacht, smaller and faster than the others. It was therefore a useful ship for reconnaissance. It had a crew of 56 and carried nineteen guns. The captain of the *Blijde Boodschap* was the aforementioned Sebald de Weert. He was then 31 years old and had already gained some experience in trading with Morocco. He seemed to be a man of mild character and intelligence. A man of the world, he was able to get along with everyone.

Putting this all together, the captains of the fleet seem to have been recruited by virtue of their connections rather than their abilities. Only De Weert seemed to be somewhat dependable. The others were inexperienced, some unreliable, some troublesome and some weak. But the character of the captains was not the only cause for concern. The ships themselves also posed a problem. These were not the latest models built especially for the voyage, but second-hand vessels, some of which were in pretty bad shape. The *Geloof*'s masts, for example, were rotting and on the verge of collapse, and the anchor ropes had deteriorated so badly that they broke several times. When the fleet was about to set sail in mid-June, one ship began to sink. We don't know which of the five ships it was, but all had to return to port and wait until it was repaired. The delay concerned Adams. He was worried about the headwinds that blow near Africa in September. If they entered those waters when such winds were high, they risked getting stuck and running out of food.

The Secret Plan

Despite this disturbing omen, the people of Rotterdam were in a jubilant mood. They thought the fleet would follow Houtman's example and sail to Asia via the Cape of Good Hope. There, they would buy all kinds of spices and other valuable goods. A successful voyage would bring wealth and prestige to the city.

The purpose of procuring such goods in Asia was stated in the application submitted to the States General, the governing body of the United Provinces. Other official documents suggested more or less the same thing. The wording of these statements is less specific, but they are still written in such a way as to suggest a peaceful, commercial voyage.

However, the fleet had 107 cannons on board. Each cannon had enough ammunition for eighty shots. In addition, each ship was loaded with gunpowder, guns, bullets and other weapons. This seemed more than enough for self-defence in the event of an encounter with pirates. Moreover, there were many soldiers on board. We know this from accounts given by several crew members after the voyage. Apart from the sailors, every man carried a musket or other firearm. There even seems to have been a 'sergeant' who commanded the men. As it happens, a council of war was also set up. In view of all this, it is hard to believe that the voyage was ever considered to be one of peaceful trading.

In fact, the fleet had a purpose other than trade, which was kept secret from the public and the crew. Van Meteren described the departure of the Van der Haegen fleet and its subsequent plans in his book *Memorien der Belgische ofte Nederlantsche Historie* (1599). As a consul in London, Van Meteren was privy to inside information that was not available to the public. He described the real plan of the shipowners:

> The fleet, well equipped with everything, set sail from Den Briele on the 26th of June. There were about five hundred men on board. Among them were many soldiers skilled in using guns or weapons. They began their journey to Brazil. After passing through the Strait of Magellan, they will sail along the coasts of Chile and Peru, proceed to the Philippines, and then to China or Japan. After trading [there], they will make a round of the world via the Cape of Good Hope, and then return home.

This version of events differs from the official documents; it suggests that the shipowners intended from the outset to replicate Drake's and Cavendish's circumnavigation. Given Van Meteren's account, the heavy armament of the fleet and the subsequent behaviour of the captains, the real purpose of the expedition was to target Spanish bases and ships on the west coast of South America, to plunder their treasures and to trade some of those treasures in Asia. It was no coincidence that there were Englishmen on board. As mentioned above, Adams's friend Shotten had sailed around the world with Cavendish. This valuable experience must have been an important motive for hiring him.

The captains kept the true purpose of the voyage secret from the rest of the crew, but there is reason to believe that Adams and some of the pilots knew. Adams describes his voyage in detail in two letters, one to his wife and the other to his 'unknown friends and countrymen'. If Adams did not know beforehand that the planned route was via the Strait of Magellan, rather than the Cape of Good Hope, the difference in route would have been significant enough for him to mention it in his correspondence. In the letter to his wife, however, he says, 'And the sixth of April we came into the Straits of Magellan to the first narrow,' without mentioning the change of course. This suggests that he had informed her of this course beforehand. In the letter to his 'unknown friends and countrymen', he wrote: 'So that to fulfill our voyage we set our course for the coast of Brasil, being determined to pass the Straits of Magellan.' There is no mention of the original plan to sail around the Cape of Good Hope.

On the other hand, several crew members testified after the voyage that they thought they were heading for Asia via the Cape of Good Hope and were surprised to learn, after the fleet had set sail, that they were steering for the Strait of Magellan. Why did Van der Haegen need to keep the true purpose of the voyage secret from the crew and even from the citizens of Rotterdam? Perhaps he wanted to prevent Spanish spies in the United Provinces from finding out. Yet he failed in this endeavour: the citizens and most of the crew may have been unaware of the fleet's true intentions, but the Spanish authorities received the information through their spies at an early stage.

The source of the leak was Olivier van Noort's fleet, which left Rotterdam a month later. Like Van der Haegen's fleet, this four-ship fleet intended to cross the Strait of Magellan and attack Spanish ships and bases in South America. In this fleet, too, an

English pilot who had sailed around the world with Drake and Cavendish was on board. Van Noort gave his tongue plenty of exercise, and before the two Dutch fleets arrived on the west coast, word had already reached the Spanish side.

On 22 June 1599, the viceroy of Spanish Peru received a letter from his colleague, the viceroy of New Spain (now Mexico). The letter informed him that Van Noort had sailed from Rotterdam on 8 August 1598 with a heavily armed fleet and was heading for Chile via the Strait of Magellan. Alarmed by the news, the viceroy set about defending the coast and equipping the Spanish fleet for the arrival of the 'Dutch pirates'.

Dangerous Miscalculations

Van der Haegen's fleet left Rotterdam on 27 June 1598. In addition to Adams's letters, there is a detailed account of the voyage in the diary of one Barent Jansz, the surgeon on the *Geloof*. His account was published in 1600, shortly after the *Geloof* returned to the United Provinces. We also have Spanish records of the interrogation of Dirck Gerritsz and his crew on the *Blijde Boodschap*. This ship was captured by the Spanish near Chile. From these three sources we can reconstruct Adams's voyage to South America and beyond.

At first the wind blew from the northeast and the voyage was smooth. But as soon as the fleet entered English waters, the wind turned against them. Stuck, they anchored at the Downs on the south coast, near the mouth of the Thames, and waited for the wind to change. Two weeks later, on 15 July, an easterly wind came up, and the fleet was back on its way.

The wind kept changing direction, slowing the fleet down. For several weeks, nothing happened. All Adams could see was a vast, endless sea. This situation continued until 10 August. That evening, near Cape São Vicente, the southwestern tip of Portugal, four ships suddenly appeared in the distance. One of the four ships turned out to be a Spanish pinnace. Thinking they were Spanish ships, Mahu ordered Adams and his men to pursue them. The sailors aboard the *Hoop* turned on the four fleeing ships and fired their cannon at the largest.

The attacked ship surrendered. Mahu sent a rowboat to investigate who they were. When the boat returned, it brought the news that the large ship was an English vessel, not a Spanish one. On hearing this, Mahu ordered Adams and his men to change course and return to their shipmates. Meanwhile, the other captains who had seen the *Hoop* in action were all in pursuit of the other three unknown ships. The *Blijde Boodschap*, commanded by De Weert, captured one of them and transferred the English captain to his own ship.

All these actions were carried out in the dark. The five ships of the fleet therefore could not locate each other. It was not until the following day that they reunited, and the English captain was handed over to the *Hoop*. Mahu received him politely and apologized for the attack, saying that he had thought them to be Spaniards, their common enemy. He soon found out that the captain and his two English ships had captured a Spanish ship and a Dutch ship just before the encounter.

One would expect Mahu to be upset about the English capturing a Dutch vessel. But the captain explained that the Dutch ship was actually smuggling with the Spanish. As trading with the enemy was forbidden, Mahu released the captain. Although the sailors were ill at ease allowing their countrymen to be held captive on an English ship, Mahu persuaded them. However, he freed some of the crew from the captured Dutch ship and transferred them to his own fleet. They then parted company with the English.

As the record of this encounter shows, the fleet was battle-hardened for the voyage. Had the four ships engaged been Spanish, a fierce confrontation would have ensued. Continuing their voyage, they sailed from Cape São Vicente to Guinea. As Guinea, at the western end of West Africa, is the closest point to South America, they intended to cross the Atlantic from there. However, nine days later, on 19 August, the fleet approached the Barbary Coast where Morocco is now. This came as a great surprise to everyone, since the pilots had estimated that they should be on a course far from the coast. When they realized they drew near land, they found themselves in shallow water, about twelve fathoms deep. The wind was blowing so hard that the ships were being pushed further and further towards land. To avoid being crushed by the reefs, the crew dropped anchor.

Despite the risk of grounding in water less than three and a half fathoms deep, the *Geloof*'s position approached an area of only five fathoms deep. To make matters worse, its anchor rope was caught on the reef. To get away, two sailors had to jump into the water to untie it. The only ship in the fleet to escape danger was the *Hoop*, with Adams on board. With extensive experience of sailing in Moroccan waters, Adams had apparently spotted the approach of the land early on and steered the ship well to avoid being swept ashore. As luck would have it, the other ships also moved away from the shore, and the five ships reunited.

What caused the miscalculation? The pilots had worked daily to estimate the ship's position. Once they had established this, they used this information to calculate the course to be taken. In order to determine the ship's position, they had to estimate the latitude and longitude on a regular basis.

To calculate latitude, pilots used the position of the North Star or the Sun as a reference point. In the northern hemisphere, they measured the angle between the North Star and the horizon (altitude angle) to determine latitude. In the southern hemisphere they had to use the altitude of the Sun as a reference point because the North Star could not be observed during the day. Quadrants and other astronomical instruments were used to measure the altitude of the Sun at noon. By comparing the altitude of the Sun with the astronomical calendar, it was possible to calculate latitude. This work had to be done by two or three people, and since they had to look directly at the sun, pilots doing this work lost their eyesight after a few years. Inaccuracy of the instruments, lack of skill of the surveyor and weather conditions could all lead to errors.

Estimation of longitude was even more difficult. There was no celestial body on which to base the measurement. Data on the distance travelled by the ship from the reference point and the angle of its course were therefore required. To determine this, a piece of wood attached to a rope with knots at equal intervals was dropped into the sea; the distance travelled by the piece of wood was then measured by the knots in the rope, and the time was measured by an hourglass. The longitude was estimated from this distance data and the direction of the compass.

The pilot entered these data daily in his logbook to ensure that the ship's location was documented as accurately as possible. The fleet's logbook has not survived, but those kept by Adams on other voyages have. They contain meticulous records of the daily distance travelled, the direction taken and the estimated position of the ship. These logbooks show Adams to be well trained in the art of navigation and diligent in his work. However, the method of measuring longitude was primitive to say the least. There were many factors, such as ocean currents, that prevented accurate measurements. In addition, the inaccuracy of the compass made it inevitable that there would be significant errors, and these errors often resulted in ships arriving in very different places to where they had intended.

Faced with this crisis, there was growing dissatisfaction among the crew with the pilots' miscalculation. Mahu took the situation seriously and summoned all captains and deck officers to the *Hoop*. A council of war was held, and it was decided that the captains and deck officers should check the positions calculated by the pilots of each ship and compare the calculations between them twice a week.

The Cape Verde Islands

From here the fleet headed south to the Cape Verde Islands. This archipelago lies some 375 kilometres (233 mi.) west of the westernmost tip of the African continent and consists of more than a dozen islands, large and small. The Portuguese settled on some of these islands and built several strongholds. They made their living from the infamous slave trade.

On 31 August, the island of Santiago came into view. It is the largest of the Cape Verde Islands. The town of Santiago (also known as Ribeira Grande, now Cidade Velhaja), in the southwest of the island, was the main Portuguese base. There were sixty sick people on board the *Hoop*. Many were suffering from scurvy or fever. Concerned about the situation, Mahu thought it wise to go ashore and get some meat and fruit. He also needed to replenish the water supply, which was running low.

Having been informed that small ships carrying food regularly returned to the anchorage of Santiago between the islands, Mahu conceived the idea of plundering the food. So he sent a rowboat full of soldiers, under the command of Captain Van Beuningen, to the anchorage. By this time, it was night, and as they approached the anchorage they saw several lights in the enemy territory. Realizing that the enemy was aware of their arrival, Van Beuningen abandoned the mission and turned back.

The next day, the fleet set sail for the island of Maio, 26 kilometres (16 mi.) east of Santiago. The *Hoop* remained at sea, but the other ships anchored near the island. The ever-active Captain Van Beuningen was again the first to go ashore. Captain Bockholt, although ill, showed his determination and went with him. The search lasted all night. The two captains returned at noon the next day, but they had found no food or water. Instead, they brought back an old Portuguese man and some emaciated goats.

They immediately questioned their captive and found out that there were five hundred armed Portuguese and 1,500 Africans in the town of Santiago. In the afternoon, Mahu gave the order to set sail, and the fleet headed back to the island of Santiago. As they sailed along the southeast coast of the island, they rounded a corner and saw the masts of a ship. They found themselves in the anchorage of the town of Praia, about 10 kilometres (6 mi.) east of Santiago.

As they approached, they could see a large ship and two smaller ones anchored there. This time, Captain De Cordes of the *Liefde* and Captain De Weert of the *Blijde Boodschap* took the initiative. They each launched a rowing boat and boarded the two small Portuguese ships at anchor. These were empty, however, except for

Dutch fleet before Praia, illustration from Isaac Commelin, ed., *Begin ende Voortgangh* (1646).

the captive slaves on board. The Portuguese had already brought their cargo and food ashore. All the Dutch found was a bottle of wine, a bottle of oil and four or five barrels of bread, which were taken to the fleet.

The anchorage at Praia faced a U-shaped bay, with the town on the hill behind it, and a fort stood on the seaward side. The boats of De Cordes and De Weert were being fired upon from the fort as they ploughed through the waters. When Mahu saw this, he ordered all the captains to prepare their boats and go to the large ship, whose captain was brought aboard the *Liefde*. This ship had come from Hamburg, Germany, and was on its way to Brazil. The captain was a man named Hermann Webbe. The Dutch were not at war with the Germans, so they refrained from capturing his ship. Because they needed to negotiate with the people of Praia for food supplies, they asked Webbe to act as an intermediary. Webbe returned at midnight, with a reply from Praia that they would send a messenger to the commissioner in Santiago to discuss the matter.

On receiving this reply, Mahu realized that the Portuguese were buying time to bring men from Santiago; he held a council of war and ordered Van Beuningen and Sergeant Major Rombout Hooghstoel to take 150 men and land with rowing boats. Once ashore, they lined up in battle formation and marched towards the fort with banners flying, drums and trumpets blaring and guns firing. The fort's defenders responded with gunfire, wounding two Dutch soldiers, but then suddenly fled. In this way the Dutch conquered Praia, only to find it empty of people, food and everything else. They occupied the town for the time being and fortified it against an attack from behind.

In the face of such organized action, the sailors, who had been kept in the dark, became aware for the first time of the military nature of their fleet. It is difficult to maintain a battle formation, and it takes a certain amount of military training to do so. The reader may recall Van Meteren's account of the fleet, in which he wrote that the crew included many soldiers skilled in the use of weapons. His words are more than confirmed by this military action.

When the occupation of Praia took place, Adams was still on board the *Hoop*, so we cannot, therefore, go any deeper into what happened on land. To be brief, even in Praia, they could not obtain food. After a few days of negotiations between the Dutch and the Portuguese, the latter proposed to give them food if they would go to the town of Santiago.

Not wanting to waste any more time, Mahu accepted the proposal. He took the men who had occupied Praia and set sail for Santiago. However, a strong wind prevented the fleet from entering the anchorage; despite their best efforts, Adams and his men were unable to approach the harbour. Having given up hope, Vice-Admiral De Cordes decided to return to Praia. He sent a rowing boat with twelve sailors to Santiago to inform the Portuguese of his decision.

When the sailors reached the shore, they were confronted with an astonishing sight. There were many armed Portuguese soldiers, their cannon lined up on the beach, waiting for them. They planned to fire on the fleet if the Dutch entered the anchorage. The sailors were locked in a house and had to spend the night there. The next day they were released and sent back to the fleet. This was apparently done with the intention that the prisoners would inform the Dutch in the fleet that the Portuguese were ready for battle, thus encouraging the Dutch fleet to withdraw from the Cape Verde Islands as soon as possible. When Mahu heard of the ambush, he ordered a return to Praia. De Cordes occupied Praia again and brought the barrels ashore to fill them with drinking water.

In the meantime, the Portuguese cavalry arrived and attacked. While Sergeant Hooghstoel's troops repulsed the attack, the sailors continued to replenish their drinking water at a rapid pace. Mahu, who had been watching the battle from afar, sent a party to rescue the Dutchmen on shore and bring them all back to the ship.

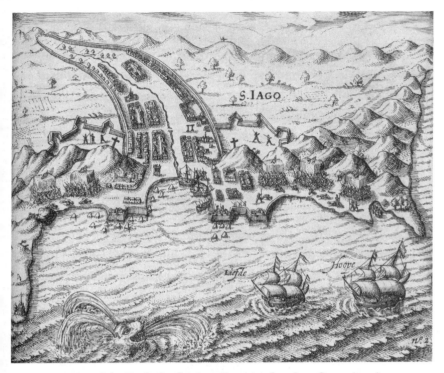

Liefde and the *Hoop* before Santiago, illustration from Isaac Commelin, ed., *Begin ende Voortgangh* (1646).

Mahu was worried about his crew. Most of them were ill, and Mahu himself had a fever. The fleet had already spent eleven days in the Cape Verde Islands without making any progress. To escape the impasse, Mahu left the island of Santiago and sailed west to Brava. On this island, Van Beuningen and Bockholt landed and took as much drinking water as they needed. De Weert followed them ashore in a rowboat. Finding a stockpile of grain in a small village hut, he plundered it and also brought on board two large turtles he had found on the beach, each of which was carrying over six hundred eggs. The crew were delighted to finally get some food, however little.

Death of Mahu

Concerned about Admiral Mahu's health, De Weert went to the flagship after returning from the island. There he found that the admiral's condition had deteriorated considerably. De Weert immediately summoned the other captains to the flagship and held a meeting in the captain's cabin. Realizing that he did not have long to live, Mahu delegated full authority to Vice-Admiral De Cordes. In a show of leadership, De Cordes ordered a survey to be made of the amount of drinking water stored on each ship and to divide it equally between the ships. As there were so many sick men on the *Hoop*, he assigned three or four to each ship and transferred the healthy ones to the flagship. He also reduced the food rations. The fleet left the Cape Verde Islands on 15 September with a northeasterly wind.

A week later, on 22 September, the flagship sounded her guns and lowered her stern flag to half-mast. When the captains saw this, they again gathered on board the *Hoop*, where they saw that Mahu had a high fever and was extremely weak. He was no longer expected to recover. At midnight the next day, in the care of De Cordes and Van Beuningen, Mahu breathed his last.

On 25 September, all the captains and deck officers went aboard the *Hoop* to attend Mahu's funeral. The captains carried Mahu's body from the captain's cabin to the mast in a coffin filled with stones to add weight. The coffin was then floated into the sea and sunk. A council of war was held, and a letter from Van der Haegen and the other shipowners was opened and read aloud. The letter stated that if Mahu were to die during the voyage, De Cordes would take over. The fact that Mahu's succession had been formalized in this way allayed the crew's fears. After the captains and deck officers had sworn their allegiance to De Cordes, he moved to the flagship as the new admiral.

In appointing his second-in-command, De Cordes chose Van Beuningen, who had always been at the forefront of events.

Accordingly, Van Beuningen moved to the sub-flagship the *Liefde* as its new captain. De Weert, who had been instrumental in procuring food, was promoted from his position as captain of the *Blijde Boodschap* to become the new captain of the *Geloof.* Bockholt stayed on as captain of the *Trouw*, while Dirck Gerritsz was chosen to captain the yacht. Gerritsz had previously worked for the Portuguese and had spent a lot of time in Asia. He had also sailed to China and Japan. For this reason, he was called 'Dirck China'. Because of his fluency in Portuguese, Gerritsz had played an active role in the negotiations with the Portuguese on the island of Santiago.

Jansz does not specify in his diary what Gerritsz's role was before he became captain of the *Blijde Boodschap*. According to Gerritsz's own account, which he gave when he was later captured by the Spanish, he was originally on board the *Liefde*, and several other sources state that he was a deck officer and pilot. Based on this information, we can conclude that the *Liefde* was left without an experienced pilot when Gerritsz transferred to the *Blijde Boodschap*.

As far as we have been able to find out, Adams served as pilot on board the flagship *Hoop*, under the command of Mahu. We know that Adams was transferred from the *Hoop* to the *Liefde* at some point during the voyage, but there is no record of this transfer in Adams's letters or in Jansz's diary. It is clear that this major reshuffle of captains was accompanied by a transfer of personnel between the various ships, so it is therefore reasonable to assume that Adams's transfer took place at this time.

As mentioned above, the transfer of Gerritsz left the *Liefde* without an experienced pilot. While the *Liefde* lost a pilot, there were several pilots on board the flagship, amongst them Shotten and Adams. The sources confirm that Shotten continued to steer the *Hoop*, together with another Englishman, Thomas Spring, and a Dutch pilot. Between the time of this major reshuffle and the time when Adams himself mentions his presence on board the *Liefde* in his letter, there was no other event to indicate a change of ship. It is therefore logical to assume that it was at this point that Adams was reassigned to the *Liefde* to fill the vacant position of pilot.

On board the *Liefde*, Adams saw his brother again. When the crew of the *Blijde Boodschap* was captured by the Spanish, some of the prisoners mentioned the Adams brothers during their interrogation. Putting these sparse accounts together, we can summarize them as follows. 'There were three pilots on board the *Liefde*. Two of them were English, the Adams brothers. The elder, William, was about 40 years of age, and very skilful in navigation. His brother's name was Thomas.' This transfer reunited the brothers, who had originally been assigned to different ships, and allowed them to continue their voyage together. Adams must have been delighted to be at the helm of the same ship as his brother. In his new position, Adams worked under Captain Van Beuningen, who had been promoted to second in command.

Occupation of Annobón

On 29 September, the fleet set sail in a southwesterly direction. A few days later, a signal was sent out from the *Trouw*: something had happened there. However, the strong winds prevented the other ships from drawing near. Only the *Liefde*, piloted by Adams, could approach the *Trouw*. Captain Van Beuningen boarded the ship in rough seas, and found that Captain Bockholt's health had deteriorated considerably.

It was not just Bockholt who was sick. The ships were full of sailors suffering from scurvy. This disease, caused by vitamin C deficiency due to a lack of fresh fruit and vegetables, results in extreme weakness and the inability to stand. The *Hoop* had almost no healthy men on board; there were so few that they couldn't even manage the sails. This had been going on for a month. On 2 November, De Cordes summoned all the captains, deck officers and pilots to his flagship. Adams was also present at this meeting. When asked for his opinion, Adams insisted that he did not like the Cape Verde Islands, and expressed strong dissatisfaction that they had stayed too long. In the letter to his wife, he went so far as to say: 'one of the captains of the fleet made our General believe that at these islands we should find great store of refreshing, as goats and other things, which was untrue.'

The other pilots agreed with Adams. They urged the captains to leave as soon as possible. But the captains refused to listen. In the end, they could not agree, and the meeting broke up. Adams and his men were expelled from the council. From then on, all decisions about the direction of the fleet would be made without them. This episode reveals a side of Adams's character that stands out: when asked for his opinion, he would tell it like it was, without trying to flatter. He was not a man to go along with nonsense, even if it offended his superiors.

Contrary to Adams's opinion, the captains decided to search for the island of Annobón, which was said to be rich in meat and fruit, so that everyone could rest. With this decision, the pilots changed course to the northeast. The next day they saw land. This surprised them because, according to their calculations, they should have been more than 160 kilometres (100 mi.) from the African continent. Some pilots had calculated 193 kilometres (120 mi.), while others were off by as much as 320 kilometres (200 mi.). This error led to another dispute. Emotions ran so high among the sailors that some of them drew their knives.

De Cordes then decided to sail to Cape Lopez, at the southern end of the Gulf of Guinea (now in Gabon), and the fleet arrived there on 9 November. The sick, of whom there were more than two hundred, were sent ashore, and Bockholt, who had recovered from his illness, was put in charge on land. Van Beuningen and De Weert went inland in search of drinking water and food. They bartered with the locals but were unable to get much.

Adams's fears were well founded. Of the sick who landed, few recovered, and sixteen died. At Cape Lopez, where they stayed for ten days, even De Cordes developed a fever that threatened his life for a time. Here De Weert was again active, hunting and catching some wild boar, buffalo and birds, the meat of which he distributed to the sick. As a result of his efforts, the scurvy patients recovered. De Cordes, who had recovered, also came ashore and did his best to encourage the sick to live.

While some recovered, there were many more who developed fevers due to the unsuitable climate. Even De Weert, on whom everyone relied, caught a fever and remained bedridden in the captain's cabin for over a month. Finally, on 8 December, De Cordes decided to leave and sail for Brazil. However, shortly after setting sail, some of the men who had recovered from scurvy fell ill again due to lack of food. De Cordes changed his mind once more and sailed to the island of Annobón before crossing the Atlantic. Situated 400 kilometres (248 mi.) west of Cape Lopez, this island, like the Cape Verde Islands, was colonized by the Portuguese. With an abundance of fresh drinking water and fruit, and safe anchorage, it would be a vital supply stop on their way to South America.

After eight days of sailing, Annobón came into sight. Gerritsz, who spoke Portuguese, was sent ashore with two rowing boats. As they approached land, they could see a large sandy beach. At the far end of the beach, Gerritsz could see a town with a church and several huts. The town lay at the foot of a mountain, surrounded by a long wall, and to the right was a forest.

As they approached the beach, a number of Portuguese and Africans came running towards the sea, gesturing not to come ashore. When Gerritsz shouted in Portuguese, 'We come as friends,' their attitude changed and they beckoned them towards the shore. He told them he wanted to exchange goods or cash for fresh food for the sick. The Portuguese replied that he should come back the next day, so he returned to the fleet.

The following morning, Gerritsz headed for land again. This time, however, the Portuguese had their guns out and were shouting for him to go back, so he was forced to return empty-handed. When De Cordes heard of this, he ordered an attack on the island and divided the soldiers into two groups. Captain Bockholt landed on the left with some of his men, and Sergeant Hooghstoel on the right with the main force, both in rowboats. The Portuguese and Africans, aware of the enemy's arrival, set fire to their huts and fled to the mountains behind the town. The goods and provisions in the huts had already been moved to other places during the night. While retreating, they opened fire, wounding one of Bockholt's men.

The town was now deserted, and the Dutch took the sick ashore and left them to rest in the unburned huts and church. There was plenty of fresh fruit in the forest, including bananas and

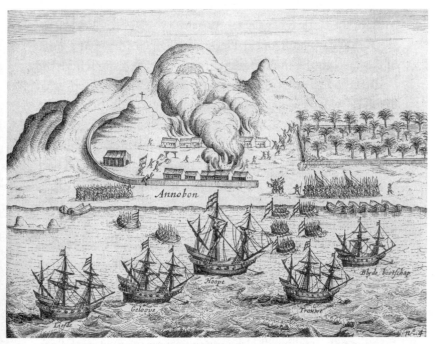

Dutch occupation of Annobón, illustration from Isaac Commelin, ed., *Begin ende Voortgangh* (1646).

oranges. The healthy sailors ran to the fruit trees and picked them with great joy. But their jubilation did not last long. Some of them were shot by Portuguese snipers hiding in the woods. Worse still, the next day the body of a missing sailor named Woutersen was found on the main road. The Portuguese had left him there as an example.

To prevent further injuries, De Cordes forbade his people to leave the town to gather fruit. To have food right in front of them without being able to retrieve it must have been frustrating for the sailors. Some ignored the order and took risks, resulting in more deaths and injuries. In response, De Cordes set up a gallows to enforce compliance. The next day, armed troops went into the forest in search of Portuguese snipers, but they found none. Instead, they brought back 27 cows. The sailors who remained in the town rejoiced, but this good fortune, too, was short-lived. Most of the cattle ran away soon after.

A few days later, on 24 December, De Cordes sent a force of 150 men to the mountain behind the town, from where the Portuguese had often launched surprise attacks. The troops tried to follow two paths up the mountain but came under heavy fire. A Dutch flag-bearer was shot dead, and several soldiers were injured by stones thrown at them. The Dutch returned fire with muskets and took control of the summit, but the Portuguese escaped once more. After raiding and burning down the two houses there, they returned with a barrel of biscuits, two Dutch cheeses and some Spanish wine jars.

A few days later, the sailors celebrated the New Year on the island. While they rested in the town, those suffering from scurvy recovered, but the heat and humidity led to an increase in cases of fever. By the end of the year, thirty sailors had died of the febrile disease. Adams appears to have been a strong man. There is no mention of him falling ill, although there were many cases of illness among the others.

Adams also landed and rested for a while. He walked around the town and counted the number of huts, which was about eighty. He must also have visited his fellow countryman Thomas Spring, who had been transferred there earlier because of illness. Spring was a brave young man who had served with Shotten as a pilot on the *Hoop* and was very popular among the sailors. Eventually Spring succumbed to his illness and died on Annobón; Adams must have been heartbroken at the loss of his friend.

Admiral De Cordes went ashore every day to visit the sick. He noticed that their number was increasing rather than decreasing, although they should have been recovering. With no hope of improvement, he decided to set sail on 2 January. The sailors loaded the ships with fresh water, firewood, coconuts and oranges, before bringing the sick on board. After burying the bodies of the sailors who had died and setting fire to the town, everyone returned to the ships and left Annobón the following day.

Crossing the Atlantic

The fleet left the island of Annobón for the Strait of Magellan. They had to cross the Atlantic in a southwesterly direction. However, a south-southeasterly wind was blowing, which slowed their progress. After about a week of sailing, they heard a loud noise, as if something was snapping. The *Geloof*'s large mast had broken in three places and fallen into the sea. The core of the mast was completely rotten; it was indeed a miracle that it had lasted so long. But there were only seven or eight healthy people on board the *Geloof* at the time, and Captain De Weert was still unable to get out of bed. If anything, the stress of the situation made his illness worse.

Adams, who had watched the incident from the *Liefde*, received orders from the flagship to go aboard the *Geloof*. All deck officers and pilots were to assemble on the ship to begin work on building a new mast. Here, Adams's knowledge of shipbuilding techniques came in handy. In order to continue sailing while the work was being carried out, the *Geloof* was towed by a rope to the *Liefde*. Meanwhile, work progressed at a rapid pace, and within a week a new mast was built using the sail girders and tethers as timber. Although the mast was a jumble of eight pieces put together, it proved to be strong, but it was slightly shorter than the original mast, which slowed the ship down.

This incident caused Adams renewed anxiety. The longer they sailed, the more food became scarce. The rations consisted of a small amount of stew per man per day, a quarter of a pound of bread to accompany it and an equal amount of water and wine. But the sailors who had recovered from the fever had such a great appetite that this amount of food was not enough for them. They rushed to eat the hot food so quickly that some of them burned their mouths, and the captains had to stand by the crew at mealtimes to remind them to eat slowly.

One day, starving sailors began to eat the cowhide used to cover the ship's ropes. Adams couldn't believe his eyes. The daily rations were not enough. On 9 March, two months after the *Geloof*'s disaster, there was an incident on board the *Liefde*. A sailor was found to have stolen bread from the galley on several occasions and to have sneaked out in the middle of the night to break into the cook's box. The punishment meted out by Captain Van Beuningen was merciless. The next day, as an example to the rest of the crew, a rope was tied around his neck, and he was hanged from the bowsprit of the *Liefde*. In the evening the rope was cut, and the body fell into the water. They left it there to drift.

On the same day, the sea turned blood red. When the sailors scooped up the sea water, they found that it was full of red 'worms' that flew up like fleas when picked up. What they were seeing was most likely a red tide, caused by the mass proliferation of phytoplankton, but it must have been a terrifying sight for the starving sailors.

Towards the end of March, the fleet was repeatedly hit by dense fog, causing them to lose sight of their colleagues. When the fog lifted and visibility improved, the five ships found each other and continued sailing together. On 28 March, the fleet encountered a violent storm that caused a crack in the bow of the *Hoop*. Three pumps had to be used to drain the seawater.

On the afternoon of 2 April, land appeared for the first time in three months. Hope rose in the hearts of the exhausted sailors. The ships moved south along the land, and four days later, on 6 April, they reached the Strait of Magellan.

The Strait of Magellan

The eastern entrance to the Strait is a large open bay. From here, a series of inlets, narrow channels, islands and gorges form a complex waterway linking the Atlantic and Pacific oceans, stretching some 570 kilometres (354 mi.). The narrowest channel is only about 3 kilometres (2 mi.) wide. Visibility is poor due to persistent dense fog. Shallow water and scattered rocks make it easy to run aground. The climate is bitterly cold and harsh. The land on both sides of the Strait is covered with cliffs and mountains. From the slopes of these mountains, a strong and cold wind blows downwards, making it difficult to stand upright on the ship. The sea is rough, the waves rolling and pounding.

Once in the Strait, the fleet headed west along the north coast against the gale. The crews of the ships had to work hard to keep them from running aground. The *Geloof*, under the command of Captain De Weert, who had just recovered from fever, suffered badly. On 8 April, the anchor line that had been lowered to steady the ship in the gale broke. The wind was too strong. The sailors frantically searched for the anchor, but the fog was so thick they could not find it.

That same night, the *Geloof* came too close to an island (now Magdalena Island). De Weert feared they had run aground, but when the draught was measured there was still plenty of room. As soon as they anchored there, an anchor line broke again. Since the ship was unseaworthy without an anchor, the crew desperately searched for it. Only with great difficulty did they manage to pull it out. Noticing that the *Geloof* was anchored near the island, Adams steered the *Liefde* closer. The next day, Captain Van Beuningen and Captain De Weert took a rowboat to the island to bury the body of a merchant named Ian Diricksz van Dort, who had died on board. Adams accompanied them.

When Adams and his friends landed on the island, they found countless birds there. Adams identified them as penguins. The penguins 'are fowls greater than a duck', Adams explained in the letter to his wife. After months of starvation, the sailors set about hunting them like madmen. 'We laded our boat full of penguins,' Adams wrote. An organized hunt would have provided enough food for the entire fleet, but with winter approaching, De Cordes thought it unwise to spend too much time there. The weather was fine and the wind favourable. Not wanting to miss this opportunity, the Dutch set sail again.

After about a week's sailing, the fleet reached a bay (now Fortescue Bay) that cut into the north coast. It was an excellent anchorage, but De Cordes did not intend to stay there for long. However, he did not get the tail wind he needed to sail. Instead, they were visited by some relentless storms. The gales often caused the ships to collide while they were anchored. Day in, day out, the sailors were busy repairing the damage caused by the storms. When the wind was favourable, the ships would be made ready, the sails would be hastily set, and the anchors would be hoisted. Then, when the wind changed direction again, the sails would be furled and the anchors lowered. This process was repeated again and again.

In between, the sailors had to row to shore in rain, wind, hail and snow to collect firewood, water and mussels. Then winter came. The constant work and bitter cold sapped the crew's strength. Food gradually ran out. They tried fishing but found few fish in the bay. On land they gathered some herbs and roots, but it was not enough: the only way to survive was to look for mussels. Those who found mussels did not bring them back to the ship but rather swallowed them on the spot. They were so hungry. There was still a small reserve of rice on board the *Liefde*, which eased Adams's suffering somewhat, but the situation was getting worse.

Adams marvelled at this environment. 'All April being out,' he wrote to his wife, 'we had a wonderful much snow and ice, with great winds. For in April, May, June, July and August is the winter there.' Often they had a favourable tail wind to cross the Strait. Adams urged De Cordes to leave, but the admiral refused to listen. In the meantime, the situation for the fleet had become even more difficult.

The seafarers suffered from the freezing cold. Few of them had suitable winter clothing, believing that their final destination, Asia, would have a milder climate. The fleet's cargo included Dutch woollen cloth to be sold at their destination. To show his concern for the crew, De Cordes had some boxes opened and the woollen cloth distributed. But it was not enough to protect the sailors' health. The biting winds, accompanied by snow and hail, were unbearable. The herbs growing on the shore soon ran out and the roots could no longer be gathered. One by one, the sailors succumbed to cold and hunger. A survivor recalled: 'At first, when someone died and was buried, we fired our guns (out of respect and mourning), but later, as more and more sailors died, we stopped firing so as not to cause fear and grief among the rest of the crew.'

On 28 April, Captain Bockholt died of pulmonary tuberculosis. He had barely spent a day in good health since the fleet left Holland. His body was buried ashore, and each ship fired three salutes. Baltazar de Cordes replaced Bockholt as the new captain of the *Trouw*. He was the nephew of Simon de Cordes. At 22, he was inexperienced but confident.

It was not only the cold and hunger that plagued the sailors. The natives who lived on the land (the Tehuelche) were hostile. When sailors went ashore to look for food, they were sometimes killed or injured in surprise attacks. By August, the cold had subsided. According to Jansz's diary, the number of sailors who died in the bay eventually rose to 120. Including those who had died earlier, only about three hundred of the five hundred men who had left Rotterdam were still alive.

Tempest

On 23 August, the fleet set sail in a northeasterly direction. Ten days later, on 3 September, they sailed through the Strait of Magellan and out into the Pacific. Blue skies prevailed. They headed north along the Chilean coast against the headwind. On the morning of 7 September, the cross-sails on the topmast flapped in the wind, a sign of an approaching storm. The sea became rough. The *Liefde* was still towing her attached rowboat. To get the boat into the ship, Adams put the bow to leeward. Seeing this, the pilots of the *Trouw*, the *Geloof* and the *Blijde Boodschap* followed Adams's example and stopped their ships by changing the direction of the bow. Only the *Hoop* continued – its watch on the mast had not noticed the movement of the other ships because of the drizzle.

Soon after, a thick fog enveloped the fleet, and the *Hoop* disappeared from sight. The remaining four ships folded their sails and drifted. Two full days passed. On the morning of 9 September, a tailwind appeared, and Adams signalled for the ships to unfurl their sails. They set sail to catch up with the *Hoop*.

The fast yacht, the *Blijde Boodschap*, led the way, followed by the *Liefde*. The *Trouw* and the *Geloof* followed close behind. In the evening of the following day, a strong northwesterly headwind came up, and the sea became rough again. In response, the *Blijde Boodschap* furled its sails. Seeing this, Adams ordered the *Liefde* to do the same, and the *Trouw* and the *Geloof* followed suit. After a while, the *Blijde Boodschap* again unfurled her sails and moved forward. Adams again followed her lead. It was already dark, and the pilots of the *Trouw* and the *Geloof* could not keep up with the movements of their colleagues. They had also lost sight of the *Liefde*, so they decided to stay where they were. Adams, who was too busy chasing the *Blijde Boodschap* ahead of his ship, did not notice that the two ships had dropped out.

The next morning the storm had died down, and it became light again. Adams looked out to sea but couldn't see the other ships. The three ships with which the *Liefde* had been travelling would not be seen again. The *Geloof*, under the command of De Weert, had no choice but to return to the Strait, from where it returned to Holland because of the severe damage to the ship and the lack of crew. The *Trouw*, commanded by Baltazar de Cordes, crossed the Pacific and reached the Moluccas, where the ship was destroyed by the Portuguese and its crew was murdered. The *Blijde Boodschap*, with Gerritsz as captain, fell into Spanish hands in Chile.

With the wind at his back, Adams pushed on. After a month, the *Hoop* came into sight. Everyone was overjoyed. The two ships were to continue their voyage together. However, just ten days later, a gale blew away the front sails of the *Liefde*. They were once again separated from the *Hoop*.

The Trap

With the wind as its guide, the *Liefde* headed for the Chilean coast. A few days later, they reached the point at 46 degrees south latitude (now northern Patagonia) that De Cordes had previously specified as the rendezvous point. At anchor, they reassembled the pinnace, which had been stored in disassembled form in the ship. Here they found natives with whom they became friends for five or six days. The natives brought sheep, for which they gave them bells and knives. It seemed to Adams that they were satisfied with this. But shortly afterwards they left the anchorage and never returned.

During the designated 28 days of waiting, the *Hoop* did not appear. Captain Van Beuningen decided to sail to Valdivia, the southernmost Spanish town in Chile, located 16 kilometres (10 mi.) inland on the Valdivia River. Adams followed his orders and steered the ship to the mouth of the river. But because of strong winds, Van Beuningen changed his mind and turned the ship towards the island of Mocha, which had once been used by Drake as a supply point. The *Liefde* reached the island on 1 November but did not dare to anchor there because of the strong winds. From here they sailed further north to Cape Santa Maria (now Punta Lavapiés). They saw many natives around the cape, and finding good ground, they anchored in a fair sandy bay.

Desiring to talk with the natives, the sailors approached the land in rowing boats. But the natives would not allow them to come near, shooting many arrows at them. With no provisions on board, and hoping to find some refreshment, the sailors forced their way ashore with about thirty men and drove the natives from the water's edge. In the process, many of them were wounded by arrows fired at them. The sailors made desperate signs of friendship. Eventually the natives stopped firing arrows and returned the signs. Thinking the natives understood their peaceful intentions, the sailors showed them iron, silver and woollen goods that they would give them in exchange for food. The natives then brought wine, potatoes and fruit, which they gave to the sailors, gesturing to them to return the next day, as they would bring them refreshments. It was getting late, so the sailors rowed back to the ship; many of them were wounded, but they were glad to have been able to communicate with the natives. Hope was high that they might finally find some food.

The next day, the captain and all his officers prepared to go ashore. Despite his expectations, he was worried: he did not know the natives, and his men had already suffered several casualties from their attacks. Besides, the natives outnumbered the Dutch. They could not be trusted. Van Beuningen held a council to discuss the best way to land. It was decided that they would make their way to the shore, but that only two or three of the sailors would disembark. The captain took his men and rowed ashore. Among them was Adams's brother Thomas; Adams himself remained on board. He was concerned about the surprise attack the day before. But the men were starving, and something had to be done. Van Beuningen decided to try his luck, hoping to get some food from the natives. Adams watched from the ship as the captain and his men made their way to the shore.

He saw two or three natives approaching the rowing boat, making friendly gestures. They held something like wine or roots in their hands and made signs that there were sheep and oxen. Being by the shore side, the natives signalled for the Dutch to come on land, but they did not come closer. The captain did not like this and seemed to hesitate. After a while, however, and in defiance of the policy decided on board, he went ashore. The landing party, 23 men in all, marched towards four or five houses, muskets in hand. At that moment, more than 1,000 natives, who had been hiding in a moat, fell upon the sailors and slew them all. Before Adams's eyes, all who had gone ashore were killed, Thomas among them.

Since there was no chance of rescuing them, the men who had been waiting in the rowing boats returned to the *Liefde*. When they realized their compatriots were all dead, those who remained on board were overcome with grief. Losing his brother this way must have devastated Adams. In addition, the loss of the captain and 23 able seamen all at once put a damper on the *Liefde*'s chances of continuing its voyage. In the letter to his 'unknown friends and countrymen', Adams expressed his dismay: 'By this loss we had scarce so many men whole as could weigh our anchor.'

Great distress took hold of Adams, but something had to be done to ensure the survival of the remaining crew. The next day, Adams had no choice but to set sail and head for the island of Santa Maria. When he arrived there, he found the *Hoop* at anchor. The sight of the flagship brought some comfort to Adams's heart, but when they boarded, they found it in as much distress as they were. When the *Hoop* arrived at Mocha Island, Admiral De Cordes attempted to land with 27 men, but they also ran into a trap and all were killed. Thus, both ships lost many sailors to the hostile natives. But why did they attack and kill the Dutch in the first place? In order to answer this question, we need to look at the relationship between the natives and the Spaniards.

When the Spanish conquered the Inca Empire that had spread around Peru in the mid-sixteenth century, they also colonized Chile. The Spanish conquistadors were met with little resistance from the indigenous people of the northern part of the country, but they struggled against the Mapuches of the south. The Mapuches were such a militant tribe that they had even halted the expansion of the Incas. In the early days, the Spanish penetrated deep into Mapuche territory and built several fortresses. Many Mapuches were forced to work as slaves. They fought bravely against the organized Spanish army but suffered several defeats. From the 1550s, they turned to guerrilla warfare and from then on, neither side could gain an advantage.

On 23 December 1598, about ten months before the fleet reached the coast of Chile, an important change took place. The

Mapuches ambushed the Spanish army and captured the head of the governor, Martín García Oñez de Loyola. This feat led to a great uprising. All seven Spanish fortresses in Mapuche territory were destroyed. Among them was the city of Valdivia, near which the *Liefde* had sailed. The city was sacked on 24 November 1599, a month after the Dutch had passed through.

When the Dutch landed in Chile, the indigenous Mapuche people were at war with the Spanish. They ambushed the sailors, believing them to be Spanish soldiers. According to Olivier van Noort, who visited the area shortly afterwards, the Mapuches had the heads of the slain *Liefde* sailors speared and displayed outside the walls of Concepción, a major Spanish fortress near Mapuche territory. (Van Noort received this information from a captured Spanish captain.) How unfortunate that the sailors were unaware of the war between the natives and the Spaniards. Ironically, the Mapuche became remorseful when they later found out that the murdered Dutchmen were enemies of the Spanish.

Deception

Aboard the *Hoop*, Adams was reunited with his good friend Timothy Shotten. He hoped that if the two of them worked together, they could make it. First, a new admiral and vice-admiral had to be elected. Against the wishes of Adams and Shotten, De Cordes's son, Simon, was chosen as admiral and captain of the *Hoop*. In the letter to his wife, Adams expressed his disapproval of this person, whom he called 'Hudcopee', saying that he was a 'young man who knew nothing'.

Given his father's concern for the safety of every member of his crew, the men may have had an affinity for his son. At least he seems to have been able to speak a little Spanish. But he was not yet twenty, and Adams feared he lacked the experience to deal with the desperate situation the fleet was in. Meanwhile, Jacob

Quaeckernaeck had been chosen as captain of the *Liefde* and vice admiral. Adams likely agreed with this decision. Quaeckernaeck, who was 45 years old, had performed his duties as deck officer in an impeccable manner.

The new commanders summoned Adams and Shotten to discuss what should be done. Going ashore by force was not an option; they did not have enough men left. According to Van Noort, there were only thirty men each on board the *Hoop* and the *Liefde* at the time, and other sources corroborate this figure. The number of men on each ship was only a quarter of what it had been when they left Holland. Moreover, most of the few remaining sailors were sick.

Incidentally, before the *Liefde* arrived at Santa Maria Island, the *Hoop* had received a visit from a Spanish soldier. The story of this visit is recorded in Spanish documents. In 1599, the Spanish moved against the Mapuche rebellion. The town of Concepción served as a base for military operations against the natives. Concepción was only 70 kilometres (43 mi.) north of the island of Santa Maria. While awaiting the arrival of the Spanish troops from Peru, measures were taken to transport food and supplies by ship from Concepción to the fortresses under attack by the Mapuches.

A boat carrying these supplies had taken refuge in a bay on the north side of Santa Maria Island because of bad weather. On this island, the natives were on the side of the Spaniards. While waiting in the bay, the Spanish captain of the boat, Pedro de Recalde, saw a large ship approaching the south side of the island. It was the *Hoop*. Recalde suspected that this unidentified vessel was a pirate ship, and, without the Dutch noticing, he sailed to Concepción and reported it to Francisco de Quiñones, Loyola's successor as commander-in-chief of the Spanish army and governor of Chile. Shortly afterwards, a Spanish soldier stationed on the island confirmed the report. He also told Quiñones that this alleged pirate ship was waiting for its comrades, since it had a constant watch on top of its mast.

The island of Santa Maria did not have the troops to repel a pirate invasion, nor did Quiñones have the warships and soldiers to fend off the pirates on his own. So, something had to be done to prevent them from landing. Quiñones decided to buy time and gather information until reinforcements arrived from Peru. In the meantime, he sent Captain Antonio Recio to the island to supply the Spanish with weapons. After fortifying the island, Recio sailed in a small boat towards the *Hoop*. When he had brought the boat alongside the Dutch ship, Recio inquired about the purpose of their visit. After a while he received a letter written in De Cordes's broken Spanish and Portuguese: 'We are subjects of King Philip of Spain, not Spaniards, but loyal Dutchmen. We are merchants and have come with a large quantity of goods which we wish to sell and exchange for some food, which is in short supply.'

When Recio read the letter, he immediately realized that he was dealing with 'enemies, pirates, English'. He was well aware that the Dutch were forbidden to trade in America. Moreover, the Dutch and the Spanish were at war in Europe. The Spanish used the word 'English' as a synonym for 'pirates'.

Recio, however, did not show his mistrust, telling De Cordes that he was only a simple captain guarding the island with one hundred Spaniards and three hundred natives. He added that he had no authority to trade or give permission for them to land. Yet, he would make an application to the governor, Quiñones, and would bring him an answer as soon as possible. To say that there were about four hundred soldiers on the island was clearly an exaggeration. Obviously, this was a ploy to dissuade the Dutch from landing. The pretext of needing Quiñones's permission was also a way of buying time.

Just as he was about to set sail for Concepción, Recio saw another 'enemy ship' enter the bay. This arrival alarmed him. The Mapuches had provoked a rebellion, and now they faced the peril of two heavily armed pirate ships. In reality, however, the beleaguered

Dutch were no longer a threat to the Spanish. With their lack of manpower, they would be defenceless against an attack by the Spanish fleet. De Cordes and his crew discussed what to do if the Spanish captain returned with the governor's answer. First, they transferred most of the crew to the *Hoop*, so that their lack of numbers would not be discovered. De Cordes would entertain the Spanish captain on board the *Hoop* and gain his confidence in order to obtain provisions. Once provisions were in hand, they would depart as quickly as possible.

This dire situation was not yet known in the Spanish camp. When Governor Quiñones was informed that the number of pirate ships had increased to two, he became even more fearful of a landing on the island of Santa Maria. The Spanish fleet had not yet arrived from Peru. To prevent the pirates from landing, he pretended to believe the Dutch claims and tried to compensate them by giving them the food they requested. Having received this order, Recio returned to the island.

Once again, Recio took a small boat to the *Hoop*, and this time he boarded the ship. With Adams watching from the side, Recio was treated generously by De Cordes. While on board the *Hoop*, Recio observed the situation. He counted between 47 and 48 sailors, but when he asked to see the *Liefde* as well, De Cordes used various excuses to dissuade him. This aroused Recio's suspicions. He saw through De Cordes's deceptions and realized that the number of sailors on board both ships was tiny. He also deduced that there was only enough food to last for two months. From all this, he concluded that the Dutch were indeed in a dire situation.

It occurred to Recio that he could confiscate both ships if he could persuade the Dutch to come to Concepción. De Cordes eagerly took part in this farce. When Recio left, he gave him a letter to Governor Quiñones in which he wrote: 'I offer myself and my ships to your King Felipe and to you.' De Cordes also promised to fight together against the Mapuches. He wanted to sail right away to Concepción, but he needed a pilot. Recio replied he would send one from Concepción. Having said this, he left the *Hoop*.

This bought the Dutch more time. They received some food from Recio, but it was not enough. The next day, two Spaniards from the island of Santa Maria boarded the *Hoop*. They looked around the ship and then tried to disembark. But Adams and his men would have none of it. At first the Spaniards were angry, but when the Dutch complained that they needed food, they agreed to trade goods for food, including sheep and cattle. This gave the Dutch enough provisions to continue their journey. After a twenty-day anchorage on the island of Santa Maria, the sailors who had been ill were fully recovered. De Cordes, Quaeckernaeck, Adams and Shotten then met to discuss what to do next. The pilots suggested putting all the cargo on one ship and burning the other. As there were only a few men left, it would be more efficient to concentrate everyone on one ship. But the captains were not keen on such a bold suggestion. After a long discussion, the captains' opinion prevailed. They decided to continue the voyage with two large ships and the pinnace that had been assembled in northern Patagonia.

The next step was to discuss their destination. Originally, the fleet was supposed to plunder Spanish ships and towns in South America before heading to Asia, but a shortage of men rendered this plan out of the question. The ship was loaded with woollen cloth. As the climate in the Moluccas and other parts of South Asia was mild, they expected that wool would not sell well in that part of the world. Still, Gerritsz had previously stated that there was a demand for this product in Japan.

This story seemed credible, since Gerritsz had previously spent the winter in Nagasaki as a member of a Portuguese ship's crew. Hence, they decided to go to Japan. On 27 November, the ships lifted anchor and disappeared from Santa Maria Island. Meanwhile, Recio gave an account of the Dutch ships to Governor Quiñónes.

The governor, of course, did not believe De Cordes's promises, but Recio reported that the Dutch were suffering from a severe shortage of men and food. In this situation, Quiñones thought, the Dutch had no choice but to surrender. If two Dutch ships could come to Concepción, they might get some men, cannon, arms and ammunition, along with two warships. Quiñones was convinced that they would be of great help in the war against the Mapuches. With these faint hopes, Quiñones sent a small boat with a pilot to the island of Santa Maria. At the same time, he sent Recio to Lima with a letter to the viceroy of Peru to give him a detailed report. In the letter he wrote: 'I believe they [the Dutch] will be in this port within two days.'

However, by the time the pilot reached Santa Maria, the Dutch ships had disappeared without a trace. Meanwhile, the viceroy of Peru had received word from Spain of the arrival of the Dutch pirates and had prepared a fleet to defend the coast. Four warships and seven hundred men sailed for Concepción as soon as Recio had made his report. Yet, contrary to expectations, no Dutch ships were found there. After several months of searching in the waters around Peru and Chile, the whereabouts of the *Hoop* and the *Liefde* remained unknown.

3

Winning the Shogun's Favour

Comming before the King, he viewed me well, and seemed to be wonderfull favourable.

WILLIAM ADAMS in Japan to his wife in England, *c.* 1611

Having arrived in Japan, Adams found himself confronting Tokugawa Ieyasu, the country's most powerful warlord, who would later become shogun. This meeting would change Adams's life as a sailor forever and immortalize his name.

Crossing the Pacific

After leaving Santa Maria Island on 27 November, they took their course straight for Japan. The three ships crossed the equator with a favourable wind that lasted for several months. At one point they saw some islands. Adams measured their position as 16 degrees north latitude. He was probably referring to the Northern Mariana Islands. These, Adams wrote in the letter to his wife, were inhabited by 'man-eaters'. As they approached the islands, the eight sailors on board the pinnace broke away from the other ships and fled to land. What happened to them afterwards is not known. They may have been eaten by the cannibals, Adams imagined.

What motivated these sailors to escape? During the months-long voyage across the Pacific, the daily food rations may have been restricted again in case of food shortages. The sight of the lush greenery of the islands must have whetted the crew's appetite. That alone would be reason enough for them to head for the coast. Cannibals may have existed in the South Pacific, but there is no trace of them in the Marianas. Therefore, Adams's idea does not hold water. In all likelihood, the eight sailors who landed on the island were accepted by the natives and spent the rest of their lives there. Adams and his men also approached land and brought one of the natives to the ship. Afterwards he was transferred to the *Hoop*.

After the eight sailors disappeared, the two ships continued their voyage. Day after day, as far as the eye could see, blue skies and wide seas surrounded them. When they reached the position of 28 degrees north latitude, they found variable winds and stormy weather. Between 23 and 24 February 1600, Adams ran into a terrible storm, the likes of which he had never experienced before. In the wind and the rain, they lost sight of the *Hoop*. In the end, there was only one ship left. Adams felt terribly sorry. Still, he sailed on, hoping to meet his friends in Japan. But the *Hoop*, and his friend Shotten, were never seen again.

In the letter to his wife, Adams recalled that on 24 March he saw an island called 'Una Colonna'. Given the ship's northwesterly course, this would have been Iwo Jima, 1,200 kilometres (745 mi.) south of Japan's main island. They had already been sailing for four months across the deep blue sea. Many of the crew fell ill again, and several died. Their misery was great. Only nine or ten men could walk or at least crawl on their knees, and the captain and the rest of the crew were on the brink of death.

Then, on 11 April, land came into sight: they had found Japan. There were 24 men left on board, only five of whom, including Adams, were able to walk. The next day they dropped anchor in a bay. The ship is thought to have landed in a fishing village called Sashiu on Usuki Bay, about 10 kilometres (6 mi.) north of the castle town of Usuki. Usuki was a small fief in the Bungo region, on the eastern side of Kyushu Island (now Oita Prefecture).

Stranded in Feudal Japan

After a long journey of almost five months from Santa Maria, Adams arrived in Japan, but he had no strength left to rejoice. Looking out of the ship, he saw many boats approaching, and the next thing he knew, scores of people had climbed aboard. Adams and his men were unable to resist them and so looked on in amazement. These people wore a sort of loose, short hemp robe that they later learned was called *kosode*, kept together with a waistband (*obi*). Some even left their upper body uncovered, wearing only loincloths or short trousers. Most had their crown shaved and their hair tied over the top of their heads. The Japanese who came on board did not harm Adams and his men, but they stole everything they could from the sailors. Some of them tried to communicate, but Adams could not understand a word. He felt helpless.

The next day, soldiers boarded the ship. They wore the same kind of *kosode*, but of better quality, and had the same hairstyle. However, they differed from the villagers in the weapons they carried: a long sword and a short sword tucked into their waistbands. For the occasion, they probably carried spears in their hands. Their presence deterred the villagers from stealing. A few days later, the *Liefde* was towed by tugboats to a nearby anchorage. This was probably near the mouth of the Usuki River, overlooked by Usuki Castle. There Adams and his men were to remain until the 'king' decided what to do with them. This king, Tokugawa Ieyasu, was then in Osaka, far from Kyushu.

While they waited, they obtained permission from the local lord to bring the sick captain and crew ashore. They were also given a house to stay in and refreshments. What Adams calls a 'house' in his letter may not have represented much. In his account of sixteenth-century Japan, the Jesuit Rodrigues described the peasants' houses as mean and miserable in every way. By contrast,

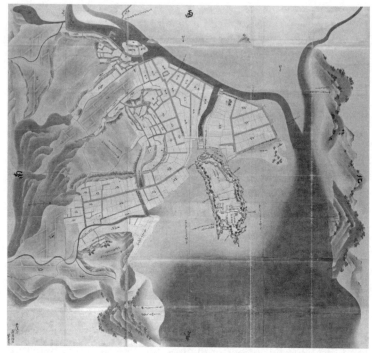

Pictorial map of Usuki Castle in Bungo, 1644. The right side of the map faces north.

the whitewashed walls of Usuki Castle, however modest, towered in grandeur over the small castle town. Still, having a roof over their heads and plenty of food and water was a most welcome treatment for the emaciated sailors. Despite the Japanese hospitality, three of the crew died the day after their arrival. Another three were ill for a long time and eventually died. The remaining eighteen recovered.

Adams and his companions found themselves under the protection of Ōta Kazuyoshi, lord of Usuki Castle. This Kazuyoshi had lived through the troubled times of the Sengoku (Warring States) period. During this period, Japan was divided into nearly two hundred domains. These were constantly changing in size and influence: some were large and powerful, others small and dependent on other domains. The authority of the emperor in the capital,

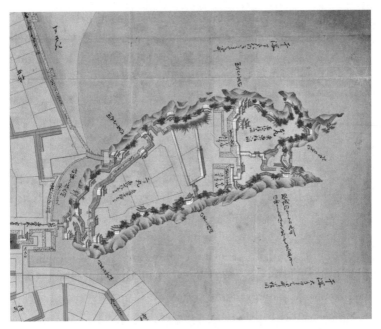

Detail of pictorial map showing the island of Nyū-jima and Usuki Castle, with the upper side of the map pointing north.

Kyoto, did not exist. The domains fought each other without end, and there was also a great deal of internal strife.

The wars were fought by warlords (*bushō*) and their samurai, fierce warriors for whom honour was as important as territorial gains. During the sixteenth century, some great warlords emerged and pacified large areas, and they extended their influence to the surrounding fiefs. After endless wars, Oda Nobunaga brought much of the realm under his control. Yet at the height of his power in 1582, one of his generals, Akechi Mitsuhide, betrayed him and killed him.

Mitsuhide, in turn, was slain by another of Nobunaga's generals, Toyotomi Hideyoshi. This warlord established his rule over most of the realm. He was opposed in the east by his greatest rival, Tokugawa Ieyasu. They were deadlocked, but Hideyoshi forced Ieyasu to accept his authority. In 1598, two years before Adams arrived in Japan, Hideyoshi died of illness. He left behind a council of five elders (*tairō*), with Ieyasu as primus inter pares. Their main task was to look after Hideyoshi's young son, Hideyori, until he was old enough to succeed him. The first action the elders took was to recall Hideyoshi's army from Korea. Hideyoshi had invaded the peninsula in 1592 and again in 1597, but upon his death, there was no reason to keep his troops there.

In addition to the council of elders, five ministers (*bugyō*) administered Hideyoshi's former lands. After his death, they continued their duties in the name of Hideyori. These ministers had their own domains, though smaller than those of the elders. The most notable of these was Ishida Mitsunari. This shrewd warrior served Hideyoshi as a page and later became one of his generals and close advisors. He possessed a fairly large domain in Ōmi, near Kyoto. Mitsunari did not trust Ieyasu and wanted to get rid of him to restore the balance of power.

A descendant of the Ōta clan in Minō, central Japan, Kazuyoshi served the Toyotomi clan. Together with his friend Mitsunari, he took part in the Korean invasion as a military overseer. In recognition of his efforts in the war, he became the lord of Usuki Castle. In him, we find the traits of a fierce general who cherishes the old ideals of the warrior class.

Shortly after the *Liefde* arrived in Sashiu, Kazuyoshi received a report of an unknown ship drifting ashore. He also heard that the villagers had boarded it and were stealing. In medieval Japan, when a ship washed ashore, the ship and its cargo were considered the property of the local inhabitants. It was not uncommon for the local lords to claim the right to plunder as well. Yet this only applied if there were no survivors (hence castaways were often murdered).

This was not unique to Japan; similar customary laws existed in Europe. In Japan, however, Hideyoshi revised this custom. To bring peace to the seas, he first issued an edict against piracy in 1588. Then, in 1592, he enacted the 'Various Laws on Sea Routes' (*kairo shohatto*). This code stated that, in the event of a shipwreck, both the ship and its cargo had to be returned to the shipowner, regardless of whether there were any survivors. The arrival of the *Liefde* in Japan took place only eight years after the enactment of these laws. It depended on the local lord whether the laws were obeyed: some didn't bother, while other, more loyal lords observed them faithfully.

In accordance with Hideyoshi's law, Kazuyoshi immediately sent soldiers to Sashiu to interdict the thieves and protect the ship and its cargo. He then towed the ship to the Usuki anchorage. At first sight, he must have been puzzled. He had never seen a ship like this before. The Portuguese, who had been trading in Japan since the 1540s, came with ships of a different type, bigger but not full of cannon like this one. There were only a few men on board, all of them exhausted, and they didn't speak Japanese. The ship was full of weapons and ammunition. The soldiers could find some merchandise on board, but not much. Certainly not the amount of goods the Portuguese used to bring to Japan. And none of them looked like merchants, dressed in fine clothes, with servants and luxurious personal belongings, like the Portuguese. Nor did they look like the Jesuit priests who had come to Japan since 1549 and converted many Japanese before Hideyoshi issued an edict of expulsion against them in 1587. They looked more like soldiers.

Obviously, this was a warship and not a merchant vessel. Kazuyoshi must have wondered what on earth they were: armed traders, soldiers or perhaps pirates. To report on this mysterious vessel, he wrote a letter to Terasawa Hirotaka.

Hirotaka, lord of the Karatsu domain in the Hizen province in northwestern Kyushu, was appointed governor of Nagasaki by Hideyoshi in 1592, and entrusted with the task of suppressing the Christians. A man of strict character, he forthwith destroyed the Christian church and expelled the Jesuits from the city. But he soon realized that expelling the Jesuits could mean the loss of trade with the Portuguese, as most Portuguese traders tended to follow the priests. So he changed his mind early on and allowed the Catholics some freedom. The governor even persuaded Hideyoshi to tolerate the Jesuits in Nagasaki in order to maintain trade relations with the Portuguese. Hirotaka's mediation skills also led to his involvement in the preparations for the invasion of Korea and the peace negotiations. He thus came to play a leading role in Hideyoshi's foreign relations.

After Hideyoshi's death, Hirotaka aligned himself with Ieyasu and continued to act as an intermediary in foreign relations. It was therefore natural for Kazuyoshi to notify Hirotaka of the arrival of the *Liefde*. When Hirotaka received Kazuyoshi's letter, he sent inspectors to Usuki to examine the ship. They made an inventory of the ship's cargo. It turned out that the ship was carrying eleven large boxes of coarse woollen cloth, a box of four hundred necklaces of coral beads, a box of amber, a box of coloured glass, some mirrors and glasses, and many children's flutes, the latter probably as a kind of souvenir. The ship also carried 2,000 silver coins.

This inventory shows that the *Liefde* carried woollen cloth as its chief commodity. This was an expensive product, and eleven large boxes would have been worth a considerable amount of money. Coral beads and amber also fetched a fair price. The rest of the goods were not worth much, making the volume of cargo tiny in relation to the total capacity of the ship's hold. The 2,000 silver coins provided some cash to buy goods, but it seemed a small sum for such a large project. Was the empty space in the hold intended to store goods looted in South America?

In stark contrast to the paucity of merchandise in the hold was the number of weapons on board. According to the inventory, there were nineteen large metal cannon, as well as several smaller cannon, five hundred muskets, 5,000 rounds of shells, three hundred of chain shot, fifty quintals (2,268 kilograms, or 5,000 lb) of gunpowder, three boxes of chain mail, three boxes with suits of armour or cuirasses, and 355 arrows, clearly intended for attacking other ships. In addition, they found a large quantity of nails, iron, axes, ploughs, hoes and other tools. These were all tools used to build fences, moats and forts for defence. The inventory confirmed the contents of Kazuyoshi's letter: the crewmembers of this unknown ship were no ordinary merchants, as they would have the Japanese believe by their gestures. With this verdict, Hirotaka officially seized the ship and its cargo.

Jesuit Slander

By the time the *Liefde* arrived in Japan, the Jesuits had already been active in the country for fifty years. In particular, they had established a strong base in Kyushu. Despite Hideyoshi's edict of expulsion, most of the Jesuits did not leave Japan but rather went to ground. When the priests realized that the ban was not strictly enforced, they came out of hiding and resumed their missionary work.

Eventually the Jesuits were allowed to preach in Nagasaki. The influence of Portuguese merchants made this possible, since the Chinese raw silk that the Portuguese imported each year from Macao to Nagasaki was vital to the domestic clothing industry. Hideyoshi stepped up the repression of the Christians on several occasions, but each time the actual crackdown did not last long because he wanted to maintain the Portuguese trade. Although the Jesuits were officially expelled, more than a hundred clerics remained active in Japan during the 1590s. After Hideyoshi's death, the edict was maintained, but its enforcement became even more lax. Ieyasu, who had become the de facto ruler of the country in 1600, showed a more tolerant attitude towards the Christian faith. The governor of Nagasaki responded by inviting Christians and Jesuits to live freely in Nagasaki as they saw fit. With this assurance, the Jesuits resumed their activities, not only in Nagasaki but in the Kyushu region. The mendicant orders, especially the Franciscans from the Spanish Philippines, also preached openly again.

There was a strong Christian community in Bungo during the lifetime of the Christian warlord Ōtomo Sōrin. The Jesuits reported that there were about 15,000 Christians at that time. The community survived after the fall of the Ōtomo clan, and many Christians lived in the area around Usuki Castle, Sōrin's former stronghold. After Sōrin's death, Bungo was split up into a number of smaller domains. As a result, the Christians who lived there were divided among different lords. As none of these lords was a Christian, the Jesuits were not very active in the area. A Jesuit, with a friar and some assistants, travelled around the area from time to time, visiting the local Christians and organizing religious services.

On one of their routine trips, they heard that an unknown Western ship had drifted into Usuki Bay. Thinking it was a Spanish vessel sailing between Mexico and the Philippines, they rushed to the castle town. Five or six days after Adams and his men had stranded there, the Jesuit priest and his retinue arrived in Usuki. The local Christians told them that the ship carried some woollen cloth and other rare items, but also a large quantity of cannon and guns. When they entered the house where Adams and his men stayed, they were horrified to learn that the foreigners were 'heretics'.

The Jesuit and his party at once left the place and went to the castle. There, they insisted that the castaways were pirates. The story that they had come to Japan to trade was absurd. The lord of Usuki Castle, Kazuyoshi, believed that the Dutch ship had been on its way to another destination, but had been swept to Japan by a storm. When he heard the Jesuits' claim, the large quantity of weapons in the ship's cargo came to his mind. The crew of this mysterious ship might indeed be pirates, he concluded.

The Jesuits also incited the common people against Adams and his men. These castaways were pirates and should be executed, they told them. Day after day, they worked feverishly to vilify Adams and his companions. For the castaways, the hostility of the locals became unbearable. The Jesuit actions struck Adams with fear. In the letter to his wife, he wrote that their 'report caused the governors and common people to think evil of us in such manner that we looked always when we should be set upon crosses, which is the execution in this land for thievery and some other crimes'.

Two sailors succumbed to the pressure. In an attempt to save their lives, they betrayed the others and sided with the Jesuits. One of them was Gisbert de Koning from Middelburg, who pretended to be a merchant in charge of all the goods. The other was Jan Abelszoon from Oudewater. These traitors sought all possible ways to get the goods into their hands and informed the Jesuits of everything that had happened on their voyage. The slander of the Jesuits, the public outcry and the betrayal of friends made Adams's situation worse as time went on.

The Jesuits' efforts did not end there. They also sent a letter to their counterparts in Nagasaki. In 1600, there were thirty priests living there, including Alessandro Valignano, Visitor General in Japan. He took the incident of the Dutch ship's arrival seriously. The Jesuits had benefited from Portugal's trade monopoly. Now their position was threatened by the arrival of the Protestants. Ieyasu, like Hideyoshi, had no mercy for pirates. At all costs, the Dutch and English who had washed ashore were to be declared pirates and put to death. This would set a good example and no more ships would come from those countries.

The Portuguese sent a letter to Hirotaka claiming that the ship belonged to pirates, enemies of the Portuguese and all Christians. Shortly after this letter was delivered, Hirotaka received a report from the inspector and an inventory of the cargo. All the information gathered confirmed the suspicion that Adams and his men were pirates. Hirotaka wrote a report and sent it to Ieyasu. All that remained was to await his verdict.

Tenkadono Ieyasu

When the *Liefde* arrived in Bungo, Ieyasu was staying at Osaka Castle. He was already 57 years old. Born in the year of 1543, as the son of Matsudaira Hirotada, he had survived the troubled times of the Sengoku period. The Matsudaira were warlords who held power in the western part of Mikawa (now in Aichi Prefecture). They had to deal with the Oda clan on their western flank and the powerful Imagawa clan on their eastern side. At the age of six, Ieyasu was captured by the Oda clan. Two years later, his father was killed by a vassal. Soon after, he was taken hostage by the Imagawa clan and spent his youth in Sunpu Castle, the Imagawa's stronghold.

At the age of sixteen, Ieyasu married an Imagawa woman, Lady Tsukiyama, and entered the service of Imagawa Yoshimoto. The following year he fought his first battle. In 1560, Yoshimoto invaded Oda's territory in Owari (present-day western Aichi). Ieyasu fought alongside the Imagawa forces, but when Yoshimoto was killed at the Battle of Okehazama, he fled to Okazaki Castle, which had once belonged to his father. From there he fought the Imagawa and regained control of Mikawa. During this time, Ieyasu changed his family name from Matsudaira to Tokugawa. The Matsudaira clan descended from the Minamoto clan, but as such they couldn't get permission from the emperor to take over the governorship of Mikawa. So Ieyasu changed his surname to that of Tokugawa. This name belonged to a family descended from the Fujiwara clan, and entitled him to the post of governor of Mikawa.

Ieyasu allied himself with Oda Nobunaga, the warlord who had killed Yoshimoto. While expanding his own territory, Ieyasu helped Nobunaga in his battles. With Ieyasu protecting his rear,

Nobunaga conquered large areas to the west and north and gained control of Kyoto, the seat of the emperor. Ieyasu fought side by side with Nobunaga in the battles of Kanegasaki and Anegawa. In addition to Ieyasu, Nobunaga could rely on other capable generals such as Toyotomi Hideyoshi and Akechi Mitsuhide. The former showed signs of genius in several battles for his lord, and the latter destroyed the power of the Buddhist fighting monks of the Enryakuji Temple near Kyoto.

One of the greatest challenges of Ieyasu's life came when he fought the warlord Takeda Shingen, who held a large territory in the east. At odds with Nobunaga, Shingen moved his army westwards. Ieyasu tried to prevent Shingen from invading Oda's territory but was defeated at the Battle of Mikatagahara. He managed to escape to Hamamatsu Castle, when a miracle occurred: Shingen died of illness. In 1575, together with Nobunaga, he defeated Shingen's son Katsuyori at the Battle of Nagashino. In the next few years, he invaded Suruga, a territory then belonging to the Takeda family, and was granted possession of it by Nobunaga.

Although an independent lord, Ieyasu became a vassal of Nobunaga. This development can be seen in the letters they wrote to each other. Ieyasu's eldest son, Nobuyasu, was married to Nobunaga's daughter, Toku-hime, to strengthen ties between the two clans. However, the couple didn't get on well and Toku-hime complained to her father. Furthermore, Nobuyasu and his mother, Lady Tsukiyama, seem to have colluded with the Takeda clan. This may be one reason why Ieyasu killed his wife and ordered his son to commit *seppuku* (or *harakiri*, 'to cut one's belly'), suicide by cutting oneself in the abdomen with a sword. It became popular among samurai as a method of suicide to show courage and sincerity, and was also practised as a punishment. Despite this incident, Ieyasu remained loyal to Nobunaga.

In 1582, Mitsuhide betrayed Nobunaga and killed him at Honnōji Temple in Kyoto. Ieyasu was in Sakai, south of Kyoto, when Nobunaga fell. He feared for his life, since he had only a small force with him, yet managed to cross the mountains of Iga, enter Ise and return by sea to Mikawa. Meanwhile, Toyotomi Hideyoshi had rushed to Kyoto, defeated Mitsuhide and taken control of the central provinces. Ieyasu confronted Hideyoshi at the Battle of Komaki and Nagakute. Although Ieyasu won the battle, Hideyoshi's dominance remained unchallenged. In 1586, Ieyasu made peace with Hideyoshi and married his sister, Asahi-hime. She died four years later.

Ieyasu became a vassal of Hideyoshi and was given a new fief in the Kantō region. He entered Edo Castle and began to build a new city called Edo (now Tokyo). Slowly building his power base, he became one of the most powerful warlords under Hideyoshi. He did not, however, take part in Hideyoshi's invasions of Korea. In 1598, on his deathbed, Hideyoshi appointed Ieyasu as one of the five elders to support his young son, Hideyori. He died shortly afterwards. This was two years before Adams arrived in Japan.

For some time, the Council of Five Elders, with Ieyasu as the de facto head, governed the country. But when Maeda Toshiie, the second most influential of the elders, died in March 1599, Ieyasu became even more powerful and autocratic in his rule. As a result, he became known to the public as the Tenkadono, or 'lord of the realm'. He had previously resided at Fushimi Castle near Kyoto. To consolidate his authority, he entered Osaka Castle on the twenty-seventh of the ninth month in the fourth year of Keichō (14 November 1599). This castle was a huge complex with several palaces within its walls.

In Osaka, Ieyasu ruled with absolute power. Instead of leaving matters in the hands of elders or ministers, he decided everything himself. This caused more than a few warlords to turn against him. Plots were hatched to assassinate him. At the castle, Ieyasu stationed a large number of soldiers to ensure his safety.

Osaka was a new city built from scratch by Hideyoshi. The city with its trading districts lay to the west. The castle itself stood in the northeast. Just south of the castle, in the Tamatsukuri area, were the residences of the leading lords. Hideyoshi had ordered them to live there with their wives and children so that he could take them hostage if necessary. Since most of the warrior class settled in this area, a samurai culture flourished. At its heart was the tea ceremony and poetry. Even after Hideyoshi's death, most of them remained in the area rather than returning to their domains.

Uncertain of what would happen next, the lords called out their troops and stationed them in and around their residences. Osaka was filled with armed soldiers. A tense atmosphere gripped the city. But Ieyasu's main concern was the behaviour of Uesugi Kagekatsu, one of the elders, who had returned to his estate in Aizu. Wary of the risk of conflict, he devoted himself to building up his military strength. Ieyasu, whose territory in Edo was close to Aizu, saw this as a worrying development. He sent a messenger to Kagekatsu to tell him to come back and explain his behaviour.

Just before the messenger was sent, Hirotaka's letter arrived. It informed him that an unknown Western ship had landed in Usuki, Bungo Province. The ship came from Holland, England or some other country they had never heard of. The crew was small and weak; they claimed to have come to Japan to trade, but they did not look like merchants, and their ship was heavily armed. According to the Jesuits, they were pirates.

What did Ieyasu think when he suddenly received such information? If an ordinary pirate ship had drifted ashore, he would at once have sentenced the crew to death. But this was clearly not an ordinary pirate ship. Perhaps Spain and Portugal were not the only European countries that could come to Japan for trade. Ieyasu showed a special interest in peaceful diplomacy. After Hideyoshi's death, he had recalled Hideyoshi's generals from Korea and tried to normalize relations with the peninsula. Hoping to open Japan's doors to foreign trade, he also sent letters to other countries in Southeast Asia. Unhappy with the Portuguese monopoly of Sino-Japanese trade in Nagasaki, he must have been intrigued by the arrival of their rivals. Moreover, as a devout Buddhist, Ieyasu did not trust the Jesuits. His only concern was the ship's heavy armament. Ieyasu decided to investigate the case himself rather than leave it to the governor of Nagasaki, and promptly sent some galleys to Bungo with orders to bring the captain to Osaka.

When Ieyasu's men arrived in Usuki, it was Adams who answered the call. Captain Quaeckernaeck was too ill to attend to them, so Adams chose Jan Joosten Lodensteijn to go with him. Lodensteijn came from a prominent family in the town of Delft, near Rotterdam. He was undoubtedly one of the merchants on board, since a man from such a background would not have joined the fleet as an ordinary sailor. His knowledge of Dutch affairs and commerce made him a most suitable companion.

Both men said goodbye to their captain and the others and set off for Osaka. Because of the Jesuits' slander, Adams thought there was little hope of their being rescued. As he boarded the galley, he felt compelled to pray to God. In the letter to his wife, he wrote: 'I went to him, commending myself into His hands that had preserved me from so many perils on the sea.'

Ieyasu's Insight

The two sailors arrived in Osaka on 12 May 1600. Adams was overwhelmed by the splendour of Ieyasu's palace, 'being a wonderful costly house gilded with gold in abundance'. He describes his first meeting with Ieyasu in detail in his letter to his wife, and based on this account, it is possible to reproduce their interaction.

Ieyasu looked kindly upon Adams and Lodensteijn. Who were the sailors on this unknown ship? His eagle eyes tried to discern their true nature. Contrary to Adams's fears, Ieyasu took a favourable view of him. In an attempt to communicate, he made many signs; some Adams understood, some he did not. In the end, someone came who could speak Portuguese. We don't know who this person was, but he was probably Japanese, since Adams made no mention in his letters of being Portuguese or Jesuit.

Through the interpreter, Ieyasu asked Adams what country he was from and what had prompted him to come so far. Adams showed Ieyasu his country on a map he had brought with him and explained that they had long sought a way to travel to Asia and desired friendship with all the Asian kings through trade. Although it is not mentioned in Adams's letter, Lodensteijn, who was also present, would naturally have pointed to the United Provinces on the same map. By questioning them both, Ieyasu was able to learn about England and the United Provinces at the same time. Adams continued in broken Portuguese that they wished to bring from their country goods that Japan did not have, and to buy in Japan what their country did not have. This must have sounded like music to the ears of Ieyasu, who was keen to promote foreign trade with as many countries as possible.

Then Ieyasu asked whether Adams's country had wars. This may sound like an ordinary question, but it shows Ieyasu's keen insight. The Jesuits, who had close links with Portugal, had informed him that this was a pirate ship. Their active intervention made Ieyasu suspicious: perhaps the Jesuits were calling the Dutch and English pirates because Portugal was at war with them. If the Dutch and English were indeed at war with Spain and Portugal, it made sense to arm their ships. From the little information he gathered, Ieyasu gained a thorough insight into the situation. Moreover, he didn't ask directly whether they were at war with Portugal, instead framing his question as one of innocent interest. Again, Ieyasu used his clever communication skills to extract all the impartial information needed to determine whether Adams and his companions were pirates or not.

Adams answered him, 'Yea, with the Spaniards and Portugals' – but, he added, 'being in peace with all other nations'. When Lodensteijn for his part explained the Dutch war with the Iberian countries, Ieyasu must have been convinced that his doubts about the Jesuits' story were very much legitimate.

He then changed the subject and asked Adams what he believed in. 'In God, that made heaven and earth,' Adams replied. This was a simple statement of faith, a departure from the zealous proselytizing displayed by the Jesuits. For Ieyasu, alarmed as he was by the success of the Catholic faith in Japan, this answer seemed more than satisfactory. He went on to ask Adams many other questions about religion. How did these foreigners differ from the Portuguese, not only politically but spiritually? Ieyasu did his best to find out the real truth. Eventually the conversation turned from religion to the subject of their voyage to Japan. Having a map of the world with him, Adams showed him how they passed through the Strait of Magellan. A surprised Ieyasu thought Adams was lying. He changed the subject again and asked what goods their ship carried, and Adams did his best to give a satisfactory answer.

In the end, Ieyasu turned to leave. In a desperate attempt to stop him, Adams pleaded that they could trade like the Portuguese and Spanish. Ieyasu made some reply, but Adams did not understand the meaning. By this time, it was already midnight. Spending so much time with two castaways shows how eager Ieyasu was to learn from them about the political situation in the world.

After this interrogation, Adams and Lodensteijn were taken to prison. Their answers did not clear them of the suspicion that they were pirates (perhaps one interrogation was not enough for the cautious Ieyasu). Besides, Adams and Lodensteijn were not very fluent in Portuguese. How did the interpreter convey their answers? No matter how earnestly Adams pleaded his case, he wouldn't be heard if only half of what he wanted to say was conveyed because of the language barrier.

The prison in which they were held is difficult to identify. According to the account of Valentin Carvalho, a Jesuit, they were sent to the notorious Kyoto prison. But Carvalho wasn't there, and Adams himself doesn't mention the Kyoto prison in his letters, so the Jesuit's account is unreliable. The Kyoto prison was also too far from Osaka Castle, where the interrogations took place. Adams was interrogated a second time by Ieyasu at Osaka Castle two days later. If they had been sent to Kyoto in between, they would have spent most of their time travelling between Osaka and Kyoto, and would not have had time to spend in prison. Given these problems of time and distance, Carvalho's account is nothing more than the product of wishful thinking on the part of Jesuits eager to discredit the castaways.

Yet it is also doubtful that Adams and Lodensteijn were held in the Matsuya Prison in Osaka. In those days there was no concept of human rights in a Japanese prison. Newcomers were crammed into a small space and had to obey the other prisoners. Adams, however, wrote that he was treated well in prison, so it seems more likely that they were confined to a room somewhere in the castle or in the residence of a loyal vassal nearby.

Two days later, they were summoned a second time. Ieyasu demanded to know why they had come so far. Adams replied that they were a people who sought friendship with all nations. He added that they wished to have trade in all countries and to carry such goods as his country possessed to foreign lands by means of traffic. Again, this answer must have satisfied Ieyasu, who dreamed of expanding trade.

Ieyasu also asked about the war with Spain and Portugal and the reasons for it. Unlike the first interview, this time the questions were more in-depth. In Ieyasu's mind, the war between the Catholic and Protestant countries was already a fact. Ieyasu's intention in asking about the details of the war was no longer to determine whether Adams and his men were pirates. Rather, he was seeking information for his own defence should such a war spill over into his realm.

Portuguese and Spanish ships had been visiting Japan for a long time. Through their missionary work, the Jesuits developed a strong influence on some Japanese. The expulsion of the missionaries in 1587 was partly due to Hideyoshi's realization that the influence of the Jesuits on the warlords of Kyushu had become too strong. The San Felipe incident of 1596 was still fresh in everyone's mind. In that year, a Spanish ship sailing from Manila to Mexico ran aground at Urado in Tosa. Hideyoshi seized its valuable cargo. The Spanish pilot, Francisco de Olandia, in an attempt to intimidate one of Hideyoshi's aides, showed him the power of the Spanish king by pointing out the colonies of the Spanish Empire on a map of the world. He even went so far as to admit that the king had built such a vast empire by sending missionaries to first convert the people in preparation for invasion. When sufficient progress had been made, troops were sent to conquer the country with the help of these new Christians. Upon hearing this story, Hideyoshi took swift steps to suppress the Catholic mission, resulting in the martyrdom of 26 Catholics.

This incident was widely known in Japan. Ieyasu was well aware that the missionary work and the imperialism of Spain and Portugal were working in tandem, which is why he questioned Adams about the war with Spain. In the letter to his 'unknown friends and countrymen', Adams wrote that he had told Ieyasu everything. One can imagine Adams telling of the Jesuits' ruse to invade England in preparation for a Spanish invasion, and the naval exploits of the English fleet against the Spanish Armada. Adams's testimony and Lodensteijn's account of the war between Spain and the United Provinces must have added to Ieyasu's suspicions about Spanish intentions, and he seemed pleased with their answers.

The hearing then turned to animals and livestock of all kinds. Did Adams tell him about the penguins he had seen in the Strait of Magellan? Ieyasu seemed satisfied with all of Adams's answers, yet, to Adams's surprise, he ordered Adams and Lodensteijn back to prison. This time, however, they were transferred to a better place. Adams does not go into detail, but since he speaks of 'lodging', it must have been house arrest rather than imprisonment.

Days passed, but no call came. They heard no news of the ship or the captain and his illness, or of the others. Adams had no way of knowing; all he could do was wait for the next call, but even after a month had passed, he heard nothing. As time went on, Adams's anxiety grew. Writing to his 'unknown friends and countrymen', he recalled: 'In which time I looked every day to die, to be crossed as the custom of justice is in Japan as hanging is in our land.'

While Adams was imprisoned, the Jesuits tried every means to prove to Ieyasu that he and his crew were indeed pirates. If Ieyasu allowed those on the *Liefde* to live, it would be to his own detriment: Dutch and English pirates would flood into Japan. But if he executed Adams and his crew, other pirates would be afraid to go there. Thus they made daily appeals to Ieyasu and urged their friends in official positions to hasten Adams's death.

Such an approach to an already suspicious Ieyasu resulted in the opposite effect. It only deepened his mistrust of the Jesuits. At first, he did not respond to their overtures, but in the end he replied that the castaways had done no harm to him or his country. Therefore, it would be against reason and justice to execute them. And he added that if the two countries were at war with each other, that was no reason to put them to death. This answer caused the Jesuits to be quite out of heart.

What was Ieyasu doing while Adams remained imprisoned? A few days after the second interview, on the seventeenth of the fourth month of the fifth year of Keichō (29 May 1600), Ieyasu left Osaka Castle for Fushimi, near Kyoto. The next day he attended a ceremony held by the imperial court at Toyokuni Shrine. This shrine was built to worship the deceased Hideyoshi as a god. On the 21st, Ieyasu visited the monk Saishō Jōtai at Shōkokuji Temple in Kyoto. This Jōtai wrote all the diplomatic documents for Ieyasu. As diplomacy was conducted according to Chinese practices, the erudition of a Buddhist monk was indispensable. After this visit, Ieyasu returned to Osaka Castle on the 22nd. There, while awaiting Uesugi Kagekatsu's reply, he began preparations for war against Aizu, Kagekatsu's fief.

On the third day of the fifth month (13 June), a letter arrived from Kagekatsu stating that he refused to return to Osaka. This infuriated Ieyasu. At once he ordered all the warlords to take the field against Aizu. He then made arrangements for his own departure as commander-in-chief of the punitive forces. Busy with these and other political matters, he had no time for Adams.

While Adams was confined, Ieyasu arranged for the *Liefde* to be moved from Bungo to Sakai, a port town near Osaka. According to an account by an unnamed official, the *Tōdai-ki* (or 'The Chronicle of Our Times', undated but thought to have been written in the 1620s), Ieyasu went to inspect the 'ship from the island called England' himself. He checked its cargo of cannon, weapons and woollen goods. The latter he sold to the highest bidder.

It is curious to note that the author of the *Tōdai-ki* mistakes the *Liefde* for an English ship. Because of the exploits of Drake and Cavendish, the term 'English ship' had become synonymous with 'pirate ship' among the Iberians. As the Jesuits spoke ill of the *Liefde* in many places, the Japanese seem to have adopted the term.

Reunion

It had been 41 days since Adams was first imprisoned. Finally, at the height of his despair, he was summoned for a third time. As before, Ieyasu asked many questions, which Adams did his best to answer. Towards the end of the lengthy interview, Ieyasu asked if he would like to go aboard the ship and see his comrades. Adams answered: 'Very gladly.' 'Then do so,' said Ieyasu. At that moment, Adams must have felt an unspeakable sense of relief.

Adams and Lodensteijn soon left Osaka Castle. There was no need for them to return to their prison. Only then did Adams learn that the *Liefde* and her crew were in Sakai. With rejoicing hearts, they boarded a small boat and headed for their ship. On board they found Captain Quaeckernaeck and the rest of the crew, who had recovered from their illnesses. When they saw each other again, tears welled up in their eyes, for they had been told that Adams and Lodensteijn had been executed long ago.

A look inside the ship revealed that all Adams's belongings had been taken. There was nothing left but the clothes he had worn on the voyage to Osaka and the map of the world he had carried with him. All his nautical instruments and books were gone. But it wasn't just Adams's things; the captain and crew had lost theirs too.

All this plundering had taken place without Ieyasu's knowledge. After some time, Ieyasu found out and ordered the return of the stolen goods. But their whereabouts couldn't be determined. In return for the losses, Ieyasu offered them 50,000 reals in cash. This was the Spanish silver currency, widely used throughout the world. Although Adams refers to the coins as reals, Ieyasu undoubtedly gave him Japanese silver coins; Adams converted this sum into reals so that the English recipients of his letter would have an idea of its value.

Considering that one could buy a large sea-borne junk for 2,000 reals, this was an enormous sum of money, even if it was to be divided among eighteen people. The money was handed over in the presence of Ieyasu, in the hands of a certain person who was appointed as their supervisor. Unfortunately, Adams doesn't mention his name. The supervisor kept the money and distributed it to the crew on a case-by-case basis for the purchase of food and other necessary expenses.

The *Liefde* had been anchored in Sakai for some time. After a long voyage and repeated storms, it would have been in no condition to cross the sea. With no means of repairing the ship, Adams and his companions were forced to wait. Less than a month later, Ieyasu ordered the ship to sail to the Kanto region in the east. This was his domain, with Edo Castle as his headquarters. The order came just before Ieyasu left for Edo to take on Uesugi in Aizu.

On the sixteenth of the sixth month in the fifth year of Keichō (26 July 1600), Ieyasu led his army out of Osaka and marched east. At about the same time, the *Liefde* sailed from Sakai. It is likely that Japanese sailors were on board, manoeuvring the ship alongside Adams and his men. The voyage was hard on the *Liefde*'s badly damaged and brittle hull, and headwinds made the journey long. By the time they reached Uraga, an anchorage at the mouth of Edo Bay, Ieyasu had already entered the castle.

There is an interesting account of the *Liefde*'s departure from Sakai in the *Tōdai-ki* mentioned above. It says that after selling the cargo, Ieyasu allowed the ship to return home without objection. In fact, it was only going to Uraga, but people believed that the *Liefde* had returned home with permission. The *Tōdai-ki* then adds that 'everyone says that [the crew of] the ship was an enemy of the Tang ships and that they should have been put to death.'

'Tang' refers to the Tang dynasty of China. The term 'Tang ships' was used to refer to Chinese ships and, by extension, foreign merchant ships, including Portuguese ones. So the *Tōdai-ki* is saying that the *Liefde* was a pirate ship trying to capture foreign merchant ships. As mentioned above, the Jesuits had been engaged in a campaign of slander, calling the castaways pirates. From this account, we can notice how successful this campaign was. The Japanese, misled by the Jesuits, formed a consensus that the crew should be put to death. Yet Ieyasu did not yield to such pressure, even though he was almost alone in his views; he saw the bigger picture and ignored the Jesuits' calumny.

When Adams and his men arrived at Uraga, they again sat idle. On the twenty-first day of the seventh month (29 August), Ieyasu led his troops from Edo Castle to Aizu. However, when he reached Oyama three days later, an express messenger from Fushimi Castle arrived to inform him of Ishida Mitsunari's treachery. In Ieyasu's absence, Mitsunari had gathered many warlords around him. They issued an edict condemning Ieyasu's actions and declaring war.

In response, Ieyasu summoned the warlords who had joined his army against Uesugi and asked each of them what their intentions were. As a result, all the warlords agreed to pledge their loyalty to Ieyasu. At once they marched west to attack Mitsunari's 'western army'. Ieyasu, however, didn't join them, but returned to Edo to strengthen the defences against a possible attack by the Uesugi army behind him. When all preparations were made, Ieyasu left Edo Castle for Osaka on the first of the ninth month (7 October) with 30,000 men. He joined the advance troops of his 'eastern army' at Kiyosu on the eleventh.

Meanwhile, the western army, led by Mitsunari, marched east. Eventually, the two armies met at Sekigahara, a strategic pass in the heart of Japan linking the western and central regions. They fought a decisive battle on the fifteenth day of the ninth month, with Ieyasu emerging victorious. The eastern army then continued westwards, attacking the castles of the warlords who had joined the western army. On the twenty-seventh, Ieyasu entered Osaka Castle, and Hideyori, who hadn't officially taken sides, welcomed him. The following year, in January, Hideyori held a grand feast for Ieyasu in the main palace of Osaka Castle, and they exchanged sake cups of peace. After this, Ieyasu did not return to Edo, but made the Western Palace his headquarters once again to manage the ongoing battles and post-war affairs.

In the meantime, Adams and his men remained at Uraga. Why did Ieyasu move the *Liefde* to Uraga in the first place? Most likely, he wanted to keep the ship and its crew under his control while he was away from Osaka. Once the ship arrived at Uraga and the cannon were unloaded, Ieyasu had no further use for Adams and his men – for the time being.

Adams had been released from his imprisonment, but he had not been given permission to leave Japan. He tried in every way possible to change the situation. In his letters he does not elaborate on the specific methods he used, but it seems likely that as well as negotiating with local officials, he made trips to Osaka and repeated his petitions there. He undoubtedly presented gifts to various officials in the hope that they would intercede on his behalf. It is likely that he learnt the Japanese language during this period, as such a skill would have been essential in his negotiations.

Knowing that the Dutch planned to send more fleets to Asia, Adams begged officials to allow them to sail to where the Dutch traded. He preached the benefits of trade that would result from Dutch ships coming to Japan. But he was not allowed to depart. Much of the crew's money was spent, and hopes of leaving the country were fading. With such a small team, what was the point of sticking with the *Liefde*? The ship itself was getting old, and it would take a lot of effort to get it seaworthy again. The crew began to question what would happen when the money ran out, and a sense of unease grew.

Finally, four or five of the sailors rebelled against the captain and Adams. The mood became increasingly gloomy. As the mutineers won over most of the others, they became increasingly difficult to deal with. They insisted that they no longer wished to be tied to the ship and demanded an equal share of the money given to them by Ieyasu, so that each could go his own way. These disputes continued for some time. After two years of being kept in the country, however, it was clear that they would not be allowed to leave Japan. In the end, each took his share of the remaining money and went where he thought best.

In addition to the money, Ieyasu gave each man just under a kilogram (2 lb) of rice a day to live on. This is equivalent to five *gō*, the amount of rice given daily to a samurai in the service of a warlord. In addition to this rice ration, he also gave a cash allowance of 11 or 12 ducats per year. One ducat was roughly equivalent to a Spanish real. The rice ration and annual cash allowance represented the minimum cost of living in Edo.

Thus, after two years of disastrous travel and two years of wasted time at Uraga, the surviving members of the crew scattered. They settled mainly in Edo and Uraga, where they married Japanese women. As time went by, some of them became involved in trading in order to make a better living for themselves.

The Shogun's Favour

After the Battle of Sekigahara, Ieyasu had become the most powerful warlord in Japan. On the twelfth day of the second month of the eighth year of Keichō (24 March 1603), at Fushimi Castle, Ieyasu received the title of *seii taishōgun* from an envoy sent by the imperial court. The shogun, which literally means 'general', was the military leader of Japan. The title was originally given to the general who led the Japanese forces against the Ainus in the north. But in the twelfth century, Minamoto Yoritomo became shogun for life. From then on, the title was passed from father to son. In the fourteenth century, the Ashikaga clan took over, but they were overthrown in the sixteenth century. Nobunaga showed no interest in the title and Hideyoshi made himself *kanpaku* (regent), a position above the shogun and close to the emperor, who himself had no real power. Ieyasu was from the Minamoto clan, so he was happy to accept the position. However, after only two years, he passed the title on to his son Hidetada, while retaining the actual power as *ōgosho* (retired leader).

Adams settled in Edo, and was summoned by Ieyasu on several occasions. Ieyasu moved to Fushimi Castle in 1601, but he often visited Edo, staying for several months at a time. On these occasions he had plenty of time to meet Adams. Ieyasu seemed to enjoy talking to him about various subjects.

On one occasion, he asked Adams to build him a small ship. During his apprenticeship with Master Diggins, Adams would no doubt have had some experience of shipbuilding. But Adams prided himself on his skills as a pilot and replied that he was not a carpenter and had no knowledge of the trade. Ieyasu urged him to try anyway. 'If it be not good, it is no matter,' he said.

At Ieyasu's request, Adams gathered together his former crew members and, with the help of Japanese carpenters, set about building the ship. The *Keichō Kenmon-shū* (Collection of Observations in the Keichō Era, 1596–1615) gives a detailed description of how the ship was built. Written by Miura Jōshin, a former retainer (a warrior who serves a feudal lord, called *kashin* in Japanese) of the warlord Hōjō Ujimasa and author of many books, *Keichō Kenmon-shū* is a valuable source of information on the manners and customs of the time. According to Jōshin, the shipbuilding took place at Ito in Izu Province, where a river flows into the beach. They laid logs on the beach near the mouth of the river and built the ship on them. When they were nearing completion, they dug up the sand to form a moat and gradually lowered the logs underneath. In this way the ship could be placed in the moat. When they had finished building the ship, they dammed up the edge of the river and the water from the river poured into the moat, making the ship float in the water and pushing it out to sea.

This is how Adams and his men built a Western-style sailing ship. It was such a huge undertaking that Jōshin thought it important to record. The efforts resulted in a ship of 80 tonnes, much smaller than the *Liefde*, which weighed about 300 tonnes. Judging from the size of the 150-tonne *Blijde Boodschap*, which had a crew of 56, Adams's ship could probably have carried about thirty to forty men.

Whatever the size of the ship, we can assume that Ieyasu's intention was to pass on Adams's skills to the Japanese ship-builders. That the former crew of the *Liefde* and the Japanese worked together to complete the vessel is significant in itself. Especially in that sense, the project was a tremendous success. Adams made one or two short voyages in this ship. She eventually anchored in an inlet of the Asakusa River, which was the name given to the Sumida River that runs through Edo from the Azuma Bridge to the Asakusa Bridge.

When Ieyasu heard of its completion, he came all the way to inspect it. Upon boarding, he was very pleased with what he saw. This achievement made Adams a highly respected man. From then on, Ieyasu gave him several gifts and ordered him to be at his side at all times. He also increased Adams's annual stipend to 70 ducats, which was not a big sum of money, but more than the average samurai received.

Adams thus came into Ieyasu's favour and acted as his tutor. He taught him the rudiments of geometry, mathematics and other subjects. Ieyasu, who had always shown a keen interest in learning, was delighted and grew closer to him. So much did he respect Adams that he would not contradict anything Adams told him, as Adams recorded in his letter to his 'unknown friends and country-men'. In this way, the warlord and the pilot established their unshakable relationship of trust.

Adams most likely met his Japanese wife during this period. Little is known about her; the only information we can glean with any certainty is that she was a 'principal woman' (according to the English consul in Seville, who heard this from some members of a Japanese embassy when they arrived in Spain in 1614) and that she and her family were Catholic. A 'principal woman' is thought to refer to a member of the warrior class. Given his special relationship with Ieyasu, it can be inferred that she was introduced to him by Ieyasu himself. Some biographies refer to the daughter of a certain Magome Kageyu, called Yuki, but there are no sources to support this claim. Whoever she was, the English sources give the impression of a caring and strong-willed woman. Her stubborn but gentle nature made her a good match for Adams. They had two children, a boy named Joseph and a girl named Susanna.

Catholic Persuasions

The presence of the *Liefde*'s crew had not gone unnoticed by the missionaries. While Adams and his shipmates resided in Uraga in 1601, a Franciscan friar called Juan de Madrid, who was doing missionary work nearby, went to Uraga and approached them. Convinced that he could convert these 'heretics', he engaged in a conversation, and after some small talk, the subject turned to religion. The friar brought up the subject of miracles in order to prove the validity of the Catholic faith. His sermon became more and more heated as he showed no signs of being able to convince the castaways. At last, he offered to perform a miracle himself.

Boldly, he asked if they would like him to move a big tree across the water from the top of one mountain to another – or if they would have him remove the whole mountain itself. He offered to make the sun stand still in the sky, as it did in Joshua's day, or to walk on water, as St Peter did. But Adams told him he did not believe he could do any of these things. He did not doubt that the power of God could do these and other, greater things, but he firmly believed that all miracles had long since ceased, and that those of later times were only fictions.

Yet the friar did not back down. The next day, he said, he would walk from headland to headland across the sea without getting his feet wet. Then he set off for the town, where he announced the impending miracle so well that everyone knew about it. At the appointed time, the governor of the town and thousands of people gathered on the beach to watch the event.

The friar appeared on the scene with a confident look on his face. First, he spoke through an interpreter to the crowd that had gathered. Next, he said something to Adams and the others in Spanish. Then he tied a piece of wood in the shape of a cross to his body, stretching from his belt to both feet. Anyone who could swim would be able to stay afloat with such a large piece of wood. The friar waded into the water, but in spite of his cunning, he began to drown when the bottom was too deep for his feet to reach. The Japanese and Dutch immediately rushed to his rescue in several small boats. Melchior van Santvoort was the first to arrive. When he pulled him out of the water, the friar looked terribly confused. The spectators on the beach could not stop laughing.

On the morning after, Adams went to visit this friar to see what he would say. He found him sick in bed. When Adams entered the room, the friar reproached him for his disbelief, 'For had you but believed that I could have done it, I had surely accomplished it.' 'But,' said Adams, 'I told you before that I did not believe you could do it, and now I have better occasion to be of the same opinion still.' Humiliated, the friar left Japan and went to Manila, the Spanish stronghold in Asia, where he seems to have been disciplined by the bishop. Rumours of this 'miracle monger' persisted in Japan well into the 1610s.

The Jesuits were quick to criticize the Franciscans for this reckless act. They too took issue with Adams's presence. After their unsuccessful campaign to have the crew of the *Liefde* executed as pirates, they changed tactics and tried to gain Adams's trust.

Not long after Adams was released from confinement in 1600, Pedro Morejón, a Spanish Jesuit who was doing missionary work in Osaka, paid him a visit. Having been imprisoned for over forty days, Adams must have found it liberating to talk to someone. So, he told him about the Dutch plans to expand directly into Asia. The Dutch had sent several fleets through the Northeast Passage, along the Arctic coast of Russia, in the hope of finding a shortcut to Asia, but each time their plans were frustrated by the bitter cold. Adams also mentioned the English efforts to explore the Northwest Passage, a sea route along the northern coast of present-day Canada, but like the Dutch, they didn't succeed.

As a pilot, the Northern Passage was Adams's favourite subject. Even when engaged with 'the enemy', Adams couldn't resist talking about it. He also showed Morejón a map of the world, no doubt the same one he had shown Ieyasu. When Morejón saw the map, he was stunned: it showed Japan accurately, with the names of the fiefs and cities such as Bungo, Tosa, Kyoto, Hitachi and Higo. He hadn't realized that the English knew so much about Japan. He was also astonished to hear that Adams had obtained valuable information about Japan from the Jesuits' annual letters, published almost every year in Italy.

Adams added that before he left Rotterdam, the Dutch were preparing another fleet through the Strait of Magellan and a ten-ship flotilla to Asia via the Cape of Good Hope. This made Morejón uneasy. 'If these merchants keep sending fleets, you can imagine how much trouble they will cause us. God help us! For the world is putting us in grave danger,' he wrote to his companion João Rodrigues.

The Jesuit had no idea that Adams would become Ieyasu's favourite. But just five years later, Adams had gained such influence that his presence became dangerous to the Fathers. He could use this influence to threaten the position of the Catholic Church in Japan, or worse, the Dutch could spread their 'heretical' Protestant religion to the Japanese people. Before such a disaster could happen, he had to be encouraged to leave Japan, so thought a Jesuit who visited Adams in Edo in 1605. In a complete change of attitude, the Jesuit went out of his way to be friendly to the English pilot. He even offered to get Adams and his men permission to leave Japan.

But Adams politely declined, saying that for various reasons Ieyasu would not grant him such permission. Although true, this sounded like a pretext to the Jesuit. So he changed his strategy and began to argue the errors of the Protestant 'sect' and the righteousness of the Catholic religion. If he couldn't get Adams out of Japan, he could at least try to convert him and perhaps make him a useful tool in influencing the shogun. He took out the Bible, made arguments and tried to teach the English pilot the 'truth'. But Adams wasn't having any of it; quoting the Bible as well, he gave him a lesson of his own. Undeterred, the Jesuit continued, but Adams 'persisted in his obstinacy, when he should have been persuaded by the power and arguments of the father'. Finally, the Jesuit decided he had wasted his time with this 'obstinate heretic' and left.

Here the Jesuits met not just a sailor, but a self-taught, highly intelligent and stubborn man. He had the courage and ability to challenge the elite Jesuits who had studied for years to interpret the Bible. From this episode alone we can see why Ieyasu, who had a keen interest in able and upright men, valued Adams.

Having thus failed both to drive him out of Japan and to convert him to Catholicism, the Jesuits had to establish friendly relations with Adams. In the letter to his 'unknown friends and countrymen', Adams stated: 'so that my former enemies did wonder and at this time must entreat me to do them a friendship, which both Spaniard and Portingale I have done, recompensing good for evil'. Although on the surface he treated the Iberians as if nothing had happened, deep down he did not forget their per-secution. Having been exposed to many dangers during his voyage on the *Liefde*, he had risked being condemned to die as a pirate. Now he finally got some security in his life. 'So to pass my time to get my living it had cost me great labour and trouble at the first. But God blessed my labours,' Adams added.

4

Shaping Ieyasu's Foreign Policy

We should also keep an eye on the pilot on Jacob Quaeckernaeck's
ship, who is there in Japan. For he is a man of good living, and is
highly esteemed and treated well by the emperor [Ieyasu].
Report of NICOLAES PUYCK, the Dutch East India Company's
envoy to Ieyasu, 12 September 1609

Unaware of the presence of the emperor in Kyoto, the
Europeans initially referred to the shogun as the 'emperor of
Japan'. The first Dutch envoy to the ruler of Japan, Nicolaes Puyck,
had a very high opinion of Adams. In his report, the envoy
reminded his colleagues of Adams's presence and pointed out that
he had great influence with the 'emperor', Tokugawa Ieyasu.

The Dutch Advance into Asia

Despite his success in Japan, Adams could not forget his homeland, and longed to see the wife and children he had left behind in
England. Five years after his arrival, Adams asked the new shogun,
Hidetada, for permission to leave Japan. When Ieyasu heard of
this, he was displeased and told Adams that he would never allow
him to leave the country. Thus, because he was favoured by Ieyasu,
Adams failed to regain his freedom.

In 1605, news came to him that the Dutch traded in Patani, a
port on the east coast of the Malay Peninsula (now southern

Thailand). This delighted Adams, who hoped God would bring him home to England 'by one means or another'. The Dutch had indeed arrived in Patani. Shortly after Adams left Rotterdam, Van Noort's fleet successfully sailed around the world, a feat Adams had endeavoured but failed to accomplish. When Van Noort returned to Holland, the Dutch were excited at the prospect of lucrative trade with the East. Citizens in the major Dutch cities set up trading companies, and fleet after fleet was sent to Asia. But this time they no longer used the Strait of Magellan. Knowing that their ships had nothing to fear from the Portuguese, they all sailed around the Cape of Good Hope, a much safer route than Adams had attempted.

As early as 1601, just a year after Adams's arrival in Japan, Dutch ships appeared in Patani. This city-state was an important transit trading centre between Southeast and East Asia. The Dutch came to buy pepper and Chinese raw silk. Several trading companies sent their ships to this port. Upon arrival in Patani, each company established a trading post, and by 1602, the Dutch had three.

So many companies from all over the Netherlands sent their fleets to Asia in such a short time that competition between them became fierce. Between 1595 and 1601, fifteen fleets with 65 ships sailed to Asia, which was a huge number for those times. As a result, profits fell. To deal with this problem, the States General urged the small companies to merge into one big company. In 1602, the United Dutch East India Company was founded. It was given a trade monopoly in Asia on the condition that it continued the war against the Iberian countries in Asian waters.

The Dutch East India Company was well funded and well organized. From 1602, it sent a large fleet of more than ten ships a year to Asia. When the first fleet arrived in Patani, the three existing trading posts were merged into one. While Adams remained in Japan, the situation in maritime Asia changed dramatically.

Kanō Tan'yū, *Tokugawa Ieyasu*, early 17th century, hanging scroll.

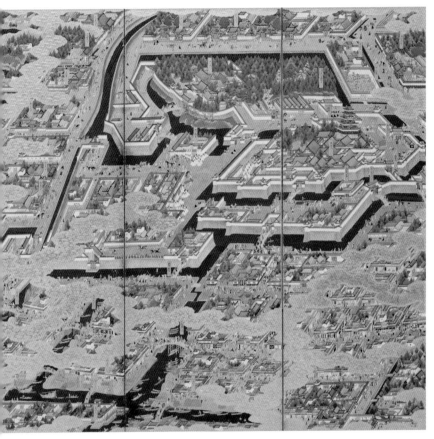

Unknown artist, *View of Edo*, early 17th century, left screen of a pair of six-panel screens. Edo Castle is shown at the top right of the screen. Directly below the castle at the bottom is a large bridge, the Nihonbashi, where Adams had his residence. Lodensteijn's residence was in the area between the castle and the Nihonbashi.

The area around Nihonbashi, detail from *View of Edo*.

Sunpu Castle, detail from *Places along the Tokaido*, right screen
of a pair of six-panel screens, 17th century.

Osaka Castle, detail from a pair of six-panel screens by an unknown artist depicting the summer siege of Osaka, early 17th century. The castle is depicted from the west, showing the castle tower at the far end and the west palace where Ieyasu resided in front. One can see the smaller tower built by Ieyasu situated between the castle tower and the west palace.

Jesuit priests, detail from a pair of Namban folding screens by an unknown artist depicting the Portuguese in Nagasaki, early 17th century.

Unknown artist, *Jacques Specx*, 17th century, oil on panel.

Japanese junk, illustration from the manuscript *Gaiban Shokan* (1818).

A Portuguese carrack, detail from a pair of Namban folding screens by an unknown artist depicting the Portuguese in Nagasaki, early 17th century.

Unknown artist, *Tokugawa Hidetada*, early 17th century, hanging scroll.

Chinese, Japanese and Portuguese merchants related to the silk trade with Japan also called at Patani. It was through them that the news of the Dutch expansion into Asia reached Japan. When Adams heard about the Dutch trading post in Patani, he rejoiced: he and his crew might be able to return home. He rushed to Ieyasu and asked him once more for permission to leave the country, but he received no reply. However, Adams did not give up. Well aware of Ieyasu's thirst for free trade, Adams suggested that if he were allowed to go, he would arrange for the Dutch and the English to trade with Japan. But whatever he said, Ieyasu would not acquiesce. In despair, Adams asked for permission for the captain, Quaeckernaeck, to leave, and to Adams's surprise, Ieyasu willingly agreed. This exchange highlights the special affinity that Ieyasu had for Adams as an individual, rather than for the entire crew of the *Liefde*.

Through Adams's mediation, Captain Quaeckernaeck and Van Santvoort left for Patani in the autumn of 1605. They travelled in a junk equipped by Matsura Shigenobu, lord of Hirado. Shigenobu received a red seal pass (*shuinjō*) from Ieyasu for sending the junk. Hideyoshi had devised this pass system and Ieyasu continued it. Lords or wealthy merchants wishing to send ships to Asia first had to apply to the ruler for a pass. If granted, the pass gave the voyage of the ship an official character and guaranteed protection by the shogunate.

The island of Hirado, north of Nagasaki, near Kyushu, provided a safe anchorage. Modern ports with quays didn't exist in Japan. Anchorages were usually bays or inlets where ships could drop anchor in safety. These places were essential to protect wooden ships from gales and storms, so the Portuguese looked for the best anchorages they could find. Hirado was the natural choice. At the beginning of the 1550s, relations between the Portuguese and the lord of Hirado were going well. But soon hostilities between the two sides, caused by the missionary work of the

Jesuits, forced the Portuguese merchants to look for another anchorage, which they found first in Kuchinotsu and, from 1571, in Nagasaki. From the late 1560s, Portuguese ships no longer called at Hirado. Eager to attract new trading partners to Hirado, Shigenobu offered the two Dutchmen a place on his junk. He hoped that Hirado would become a hub for Dutch ships and reap the benefits of foreign trade.

Shigenobu was not alone in wanting the Dutch to come to Japan. Ieyasu entrusted Quaeckernaeck with a letter to Maurice, prince of Orange and ruler of the United Provinces. Ieyasu also provided him with a red seal pass as a sign that the Dutch were safe to trade in Japan. Quaeckernaeck and Van Santvoort arrived in Patani on 2 December 1605. There they met Ferdinand Michiels, head of the newly united Dutch trading post, and informed him of Ieyasu's desire to establish trade relations with the Dutch. However, no Dutch ships called at Patani that year (1605), and it would be 1607 before another arrived. Moreover, Michiels himself was not the man to take on new ventures.

With no prospects of employment in Patani, both left the city. Quaeckernaeck was sailing to Malacca on a junk when he heard the happy news that his cousin Admiral Cornelis Matelief de Jonge's fleet was anchored there. On 19 August 1606, he joined the admiral and gave him Ieyasu's letter and pass. Matelief sent them to Holland, but they have not survived.

In the meantime, Van Santvoort had returned to Japan. The *Ikoku Goshuinchō* (Register of Documents Related to the Foreign Red Seal Trade) states that on the tenth day of the tenth month in the eleventh year of Keichō (10 November 1606), a red seal pass was issued through Adams to Michiels and Quaeckernaeck. This register was compiled by the Zen monk Ishin Sūden. He was one of Ieyasu's most important aides in matters of state and diplomacy, and his manuscripts are the only surviving Japanese diplomatic records of Ieyasu's reign.

They contain detailed first-hand information on Ieyasu's diplomatic correspondence and red seal passes. The record suggests that on his return to Japan, Van Santvoort applied for new passes for the Dutch through Adams. This indicates that Van Santvoort and Adams fostered hopes of establishing trade relations between Japan and the United Provinces via Patani.

In 1607, Van Santvoort travelled from Japan to Patani once again in order to conduct private trade. While he stayed in Patani, a Dutch ship, the *Maurits*, called at the harbour. A Senior Merchant, Victor Sprinckel, was on board. He replaced Michiels as the new head of the Dutch trading post. Sprinckel received word from Van Santvoort that Ieyasu wanted Dutch ships to come to Japan. He entrusted Van Santvoort with a letter addressed to Ieyasu and another to Adams, so that he would not lose the opportunity to trade there. Van Santvoort brought these two letters back to Japan and gave them to Adams.

In his letter to Adams, dated 6 February 1608, Sprinckel explains how Quaeckernaeck and Van Santvoort arrived in Patani in 1605, and what happened to Quaeckernaeck afterwards. According to Sprinckel's account, when Quaeckernaeck met his cousin in Malacca, the admiral recommended him for the captaincy with a handsome salary. Quaeckernaeck, for his part, wanted to return to his homeland as soon as possible, but the return ships were not yet ready. Matelief had also hoped that his cousin would earn some money before he returned, so he appointed him captain of one of the ships in his fleet. But fate was not on Quaeckernaeck's side; he died fighting the Portuguese off the coast of Malacca soon afterwards, on 21 September 1606.

Adams must have been saddened to learn of the death of his captain, with whom he had shared all those hardships and adventures. But Sprinckel's letter contained some encouraging news too: a Dutch ship was expected to reach Japan within two or two and a half years.

Having heard from Van Santvoort about Adams's influence in Japan, Sprinckel asked Adams to give Ieyasu a letter addressed to him and to translate the contents into Japanese. In the letter, Sprinckel apologized that no Dutch ships had yet sailed to Japan. The reason for the delay was the war with the Iberians. The Dutch East India Company was unable to send ships to Japan because it had its hands full fighting the Portuguese and Spaniards in Southeast Asian waters. At Sprinckel's request, Adams translated the letter into Japanese and delivered it to Ieyasu, which allowed Adams to become involved in Ieyasu's diplomacy. All that remained was to await the arrival of the Dutch ships.

Hatamoto

While corresponding with the Dutch in Patani through Van Santvoort, Adams received orders from Ieyasu to build another ship. This time he built a ship of 120 tonnes. It was comparable in size to the yacht of the Van der Haegen fleet, a 150-tonne ship. As the crew of the *Blijde Boodschap* was 56, it is reasonable to assume that Adams's second ship could carry at least forty to fifty men. In this newly built ship, Adams made a voyage from 'Meacoo' to Edo. In those days, 'Meacoo', usually spelled 'Miyako' (meaning 'capital'), was used to refer to Kyoto, the nominal capital and residence of the emperor. Obviously Kyoto lies far from the sea, but 'Miyako' also referred to the large regions around the capital, including Sakai, which was a port. A keen navigator at heart, Adams must have taken great pleasure in this voyage. While sailing along the coast of Japan, Adams did not sit idle; he spent his time on board mapping the coastline. Most of the crew must have been Japanese, although some former crew members of the *Liefde* may have taken part in the navigation. By sailing with Adams, the Japanese were able to absorb Western navigational skills. This was exactly what Ieyasu had in mind.

In recognition of his services, Ieyasu granted Adams an estate. The estate was located in Hemi (now Yokosuka City) on the Miura Peninsula. Because of the name of this place, Adams is now known in Japan as 'Miura Anjin'. 'Anjin' was a term used at the time to refer to a helmsman. In authentic Japanese documents, he is mostly called just 'Anjin', without 'Miura'. On the other hand, his son Joseph always appears in the documents as 'Miura Anjin'. In Hemi, there were eighty to ninety families who became Adams's retainers.

Writing to his 'unknown friends and countrymen', Adams expressed his deep satisfaction with his status as *hatamoto* (literally 'banner-bearer', direct retainer of the shogun). 'The emperor [Ieyasu] had given me a living, as in England a lordship,' he

Hemi village with the remnants of Miura Anjin's residence, illustration from *Sōchūryū Onkiryaku* (1839).

declared, adding proudly, 'which, or the like, were here never given to a stranger.' He thanked God for this good fortune, saying, 'thus had God provided for me after my great misery.'

Hemi lies at the entrance to Edo Bay. At the time, there was not much land between the sea and the mountains, although much has since been reclaimed. Adams's house stood on one of the hills, overlooking Edo Bay. Deeper in the bay lay Edo, the seat of the shogun. Adams had a residence there, as did all the vassals and other lords. It was located in the area of Nihonbashi Anjinchō (now Nihonbashi Muromachi). It stood near the Nihonbashi, a magnificent wooden bridge over Edo's central moat. Ieyasu built this bridge as the physical and symbolic centre of his capital, as the art historian Timon Screech explains in his book *Tokyo Before Tokyo*. The place buzzed with activity. Many merchants settled in the area, and there was a busy fish market (Nihonbashi Uogashi) nearby. Adams also had a residence in Sunpu, where Ieyasu held court. As befitted a vassal, Adams spent most of his time at the Edo and Sunpu residences, only occasionally visiting Hemi. In keeping with his status, Adams owned several *katana* (long swords) and *wakizashi* (short swords), which are mentioned in his will.

Like Adams, Lodensteijn gained vassal status, but his residence was located close to the inner moat of Edo Castle. This area, west of today's Tokyo Station (Marunouchi), was known as 'Yayoso-gashi', meaning 'Jan Joosten's riverbank', and the present place name 'Yaesu' comes from Jan Joosten's name. It now refers to the area east of Tokyo Station (in Chuo Ward). This means that Lodensteijn lived much closer to the inner castle than Adams did. One wonders why there was such a difference between the two – perhaps Ieyasu designated an area closer to the water for Adams's house because he was in charge of shipbuilding and navigation.

Western sources say very little about the relationship between Lodensteijn and Ieyasu, and as a result, Lodensteijn has received little attention. Japanese sources, on the other hand, show that Lodensteijn taught Ieyasu about world affairs and, like Adams, won Ieyasu's favour. For example, the *Nagasaki Kongen-ki* (Account of the Origin of Nagasaki) contains a detailed entry on Lodensteijn. Although this manuscript dates from the late seventeenth century, analysis of its contents shows it to be a reliable source. Regarding Lodensteijn's relationship with Ieyasu, it notes:

> The chief of the Dutch, called Jan Joosten [Lodensteijn], and the chief of the English, called Anji [Adams], were called to the castle from time to time during their stay, and when they were asked questions about foreign affairs, they answered one after the other. Jan Joosten answered these questions well, and they were both given residences and estates where they lived and worked. In Edo, the place where Jan Joosten lived was called Sogashi, and the place where Anji lived was called Anji-chō.

As mentioned in Chapter Three, Lodensteijn came from a famous family in his hometown of Delft. This may be key to understanding Ieyasu's favour for Lodensteijn, since Japanese medieval society valued lineage. If nothing else, Lodensteijn was not afraid to boast, and such boldness seems to have attracted Ieyasu. English and Japanese sources also mention that Lodensteijn was fluent in Japanese – his eloquence served him well indeed.

Although Ieyasu favoured them both, the relationship between Adams and Lodensteijn was far from happy. Unlike the reserved Adams, Lodensteijn was flamboyant and outspoken; he also didn't keep his word and often acted out of self-interest. Adams did not get on well with him, and therefore kept him at a distance.

Arrival of the Dutch

In July 1609, Adams received great news from Ieyasu: two Dutch ships had arrived in Hirado. Overjoyed, Adams set off to meet them, and when he arrived, he did indeed find two large Dutch ships. On board he was greeted by several Dutch merchants. One of them was a young and able merchant called Jacques Specx, who would become the central figure of the Dutch in Japan. Adams learned from them the circumstances of their arrival.

Both ships, the *Roode Leeuw met Pijlen* (or 'Red Lion with Arrows', the crest of the States General) and the *Griffioen* (Griffin), belonged to the Dutch East India Company. They left Holland in December 1607 in a fleet of thirteen ships under the command of Admiral Pieter Willemsen Verhoef and sailed to Asia via the Cape of Good Hope. On arrival in Asia, Verhoef assigned the vessels different tasks. He ordered the *Roode Leeuw met Pijlen* and the *Griffioen* to search for Portuguese ships near Johor in the Strait of Malacca and capture as many as possible. After some time, the admiral sent them orders to change their mission and head for Japan. The situation in Europe had changed dramatically. The Dutch and the Iberians were about to sign a truce, both sides exhausted by the long war. The truce provided for the cessation of all hostilities for nine years, starting from September 1609. Eventually the truce was ratified in April 1609 and the duration changed to twelve years, starting from April 1610.

Up to that point, the mission of the Dutch fleets had been to acquire Moluccan spices and Chinese raw silk through trade, but also to do harm to the Iberian enemy. By inflicting economic damage on the enemy in Asia, the Dutch hoped to improve the outcome of the war at home. As the signing of the truce drew near, the Dutch East India Company headquarters changed its policy. They wanted to conclude free trade agreements with as many sovereigns as possible before the truce came into force, since the status quo would have to be maintained after that date.

Under these circumstances, the merchants on the two ships received orders to sail to Japan and conclude a trade agreement with the Japanese ruler. But their mission was not only to obtain free trade; they were ordered to capture the Portuguese carrack (or 'nao do trato' in Portuguese) from Macao on the way. This had to be done before the truce came into force.

The carrack was a gigantic ship – up to 1,600 tonnes, much larger than the Dutch ships – and could hold a year's worth of trade goods. It sailed from Macao to Nagasaki every year in June or July, riding the seasonal winds, and the two Dutch ships were to ambush it en route to Japan. If captured, its valuable cargo would be taken to Japan to be sold. On 11 May, they sailed from Johor, first to Patani, where they bought some raw silk and lead, and then to Japan. However, they were unable to find the carrack on the way and arrived in Hirado on 2 July. The carrack had reached Nagasaki two days earlier.

On arrival in Hirado, the Dutch were welcomed by officials of the lord of Hirado. They helped the Dutch send letters to Ieyasu and the survivors of the *Liefde*. A few days later, officials from the governor of Nagasaki arrived. Van Santvoort, who happened to be in Nagasaki, came with them. He told the Dutch that they had to get permission to trade from Ieyasu, who resided at his castle in Sunpu. On 27 July 1609, Nicolaes Puyck and Abraham van den Broeck went to Sunpu as envoys to obtain an audience with the ruler, and Van Santvoort accompanied them as an interpreter.

By the time Adams arrived in Hirado, the envoy had already left for Sunpu. Seeing that they had missed each other on the way, he turned around and hurried back. But instead of catching up with the envoys, he met them at Ushimado, on the Seto Inland Sea, on their way back to Hirado.

There, Puyck informed Adams of what had happened at Sunpu. Three days before the arrival of the envoys, three Portuguese came down from the carrack with their attendants to present Ieyasu with gifts. The Portuguese asked for an early audience, which was not granted. The Dutch were the first to be given an audience with Ieyasu. Four days later, when it was the Portuguese's turn, they strongly accused the Dutch of being pirates, but Ieyasu would not be convinced. On the contrary, he had given the Dutch a warm welcome and presented them with four red seal passes, which guaranteed the Dutch free and safe trade throughout Japan. Having accomplished their mission, Puyck and his party left Sunpu on their way back to Hirado. Negotiations between Ieyasu and the Dutch thus proceeded swiftly in Adams's absence. Adams, unable to attend these negotiations, must have felt sidelined. However, he was pleased to hear that the Dutch would now send ships to Japan every year. He told Puyck that he would like to return home with them, but their hasty departure meant that he didn't have time to prepare for the voyage. Besides, Ieyasu wouldn't have allowed it anyway.

Puyck then asked him to recommend the Dutch to Ieyasu and to maintain good relations with the men he would leave behind in the country. Adams promised to do this, as he was 'a friend of the Dutch and considered the Netherlands his fatherland'. After this amiable meeting, Adams left for Sunpu, and Puyck and his party went on to Hirado. They arrived there on 13 September. The Dutch established a trading post in Hirado and appointed Specx as its head. Puyck urged Specx to maintain a good relationship with Adams. In his report on trade with Japan, he wrote: 'Keep an eye on the pilot (Adams) of Jacob Quaeckernaeck's ship, who is there in Japan. For he is a man who leads a good life and is highly esteemed and well treated by the emperor [Ieyasu].'

Puyck explained in the same report that Adams's influence would be of great help to the Dutch in securing favourable trade terms. There was, however, one cause for concern: the presence of the English in Asia. The English East India Company had existed since 1600, and from 1601, regular fleets were sent to Asia. By 1602, the English had established a trading post at Bantam (now Banten) in Java. The main trade was in spices from the Moluccas, and no attempt had been made to travel further north. If Adams, an Englishman, informed his countrymen of the situation in Japan, they might be tempted to go there. This would create fierce competition between the Dutch and the English – after all, they both had roughly the same products to offer the Japanese. So while the Dutch were on good terms with Adams, they didn't feel the need to inform him that the English were also sailing in Asian waters.

Ieyasu's Foreign Policy

After parting with Puyck, Adams hurried to Sunpu, where he received detailed information about what had happened during the Dutch envoys' stay there. He heard that as soon as the Jesuits were told of the arrival of the Dutch ships, they lobbied Ieyasu. João Rodrigues, a Jesuit who acted as Ieyasu's interpreter, told Ieyasu that the Dutch were 'pirates and destroyers of a trade too important for Japan'. The Jesuit was well aware that a disruption of trade would lead to an economic crisis, as Japan was dependent on imports of some strategic commodities, particularly Chinese raw silk. Rodrigues pleaded with Ieyasu not to allow the two ships to leave Hirado because if the Dutch did, they would certainly seize the Macao carrack and do other great mischief.

Despite such strong appeals, Ieyasu did not accept the Jesuit's arguments. Just as he did with the *Liefde* nine years earlier, he treated the Dutch well. Through his dealings with Adams and Lodensteijn, Ieyasu became aware of the political situation in the world. He saw that the Jesuit's strong dislike of Holland represented nothing more than slander against an enemy at war.

Ieyasu wanted as many countries as possible as trading partners. He believed that trade competition would enrich Japan. The import of Chinese raw silk was vital to Japan's clothing industry, but it was dependent on the Portuguese trade. The Japanese themselves sent junks to Southeast Asian countries for silk, but they could not trade directly with China. The amount they brought back to Japan was therefore insufficient to supply the market. In the absence of other importers, the Portuguese made enormous profits, but the high prices caused the Japanese market to suffer. To alleviate this situation, the shogunate imposed various price restrictions on Portuguese trade in Nagasaki. But as long as the Portuguese were the only suppliers, these measures were of little use.

If several countries were to import Chinese silk, this would lead to competition and a significant reduction in import prices. In this way, Japan's domestic industry would be able to grow. Ieyasu had high hopes for the Dutch trade. In a letter to the king of Spain, the Jesuit Vice-Provincial reported:

> Although the nobles and the people regarded these individuals as pirates and looked on with disgust that they should be favoured, the Prince [Ieyasu] welcomed them with goodwill and gave them permission to come to his country with four ships to trade and open a trading post.

Hearing of the Jesuit's slander, Adams must have been upset again. He must have informed Ieyasu of the Jesuits' lies and told him of the recent truce between the Iberian countries and Holland. Of course, at this time, it was unlikely that the Jesuits would have received word from Europe about this turn of events.

As we have seen, like the Jesuits, the Portuguese envoys who stayed in Sunpu at the same time as their Dutch counterparts didn't keep quiet. Yet they were in no position to stop the Dutch.

The carrack that made its way to Nagasaki that year was the *Nossa Senhora da Graça*, also known as the *Madre de Deus*, with André Pessoa as captain. As Interim Governor (Captain-Major) of Macao, Pessoa had intervened by force in a dispute between the Japanese crew of Arima Harunobu's red seal ship and the Portuguese in Macao the previous year. Several Japanese were killed in the incident, which the shogunate did not take lightly. Pessoa therefore went to Japan not only to trade but to justify what had happened. But when he arrived in Nagasaki, relations between him and the governor of Nagasaki, Hasegawa Fujihiro, turned sour. This led to distrust on Pessoa's part. He became afraid to leave the carrack and sent a deputy to Sunpu instead of going himself.

Ieyasu took the captain's failure to appear in person as an act of deceit. Enraged, he gave Harunobu permission to take his revenge. As Pessoa tried to escape from Nagasaki Bay, Harunobu's forces attacked the *Nossa Senhora da Graça* and sank the ship after four days of fierce fighting. The rich cargo was lost, resulting in turmoil in the domestic market. This incident strengthened Ieyasu's mistrust of the Portuguese. Hence, they no longer had enough influence to discredit the Dutch. On the contrary, Ieyasu hoped that the Dutch would become suppliers of raw silk along-side the Portuguese, thus creating a more stable market. Yet, even after the incident, the Portuguese kept arguing for the expulsion of the Dutch from Japan. As we have seen, these appeals went against Ieyasu's free trade policy. Therefore, actions to prevent the Dutch from trading in Japan only made the Portuguese position worse. The incident also affected Adams's status. It led to the expulsion from Japan of the Portuguese Jesuit Rodrigues, who had been acting as an interpreter between the Europeans and Ieyasu. Adams took his place and gained even more influence.

A Spanish Visitor

On 30 September 1609, two days before the Dutch set sail from Hirado, a large Spanish ship was shipwrecked off the coast of Iwawada in the Ōtaki domain (now in Chiba Prefecture). The *San Francisco* was on its way from Manila to Acapulco in New Spain (Mexico). Manila served as the Spanish stronghold in Asia. Spanish ships sailed regularly between Manila and Acapulco, the main port of Spain's American colony. Most often, they followed a route along the southern coast of Japan. This caught the attention of Ieyasu. He wanted to create a trade route between Acapulco, Uraga and Manila. Since Uraga was close to Edo, the shogunate would be able to closely monitor the trade. To realize this plan, Ieyasu lobbied the governor of the Philippines through letters and missionaries, but differing views on missionary work proved to be a major stumbling block.

The *San Francisco*, the flagship of a three-ship convoy, set sail from the port of Cavite, near Manila, on 25 July. On board was Don Rodrigo de Vivero, who had completed his term of office as interim governor of the Philippines. Caught in a storm in the waters around Japan, the *San Francisco* became separated from the other ships and was swept towards the coast of Japan, where it shipwrecked. According to Adams's account, 36 sailors drowned (Vivero wrote 50 in his diary) and between 340 and 350 were rescued, with Vivero, unharmed, among them. Honda Tadatomo, lord of the Ōtaki domain, took the Spaniards into custody. When Ieyasu heard of the wreck and the rescue of such an important person, he sent Adams to Iwawada.

Adams arrived on the scene 48 days after the shipwreck. When he met Vivero, he introduced himself as 'an English pilot, married here for over twenty years, and Ieyasu's favourite', according to Vivero's account. Ieyasu had prepared a red seal pass, which Adams gave to Vivero. This pass enabled him to travel overland to Edo and Sunpu. Free meals would be provided along the way, and the cargo recovered from the *San Francisco*, which would otherwise have been Ieyasu's, was returned to him.

Vivero was pleased with this hospitality, and asked Adams about Japan's territory. His map showed the northernmost point of Japan at 33.5 degrees north latitude, but he wondered if the actual wreck at Iwawada could be at 35.5 degrees north latitude. Adams replied that some subjects who obeyed the Japanese sovereign and paid taxes lived in places as far north as 46 degrees and above (a little north of Hokkaido). He demonstrated this to Vivero with an astrolabe. Adams's learning impressed Vivero; he described him as 'a great master of geology and mathematics'.

Armed with the red seal pass, Vivero set off and had an audience with Ieyasu's son and young shogun, Hidetada, in Edo. He then went to Sunpu Castle to meet with Ieyasu, where he was treated well. While at Sunpu, Vivero tried to resume the stalled trade negotiations between Spain and Japan. He did this without official authorization, since he was not qualified to negotiate with Ieyasu on behalf of the Spanish king. In fact, he acted out of concern for the newly established Dutch trading post at Hirado. Through Honda Masazumi, Ieyasu's close aide, Vivero presented three demands to the shogunate. These were the protection of priests, the establishment of friendly relations with Spain and the expulsion of the Dutch. According to Vivero's memoirs, Ieyasu agreed to the first two demands but refused the third. Ieyasu explained that he had already promised the Dutch protection and could not reverse that decision without losing face. Nevertheless, Ieyasu asked Vivero to continue to provide him with information on the 'designs of the Dutch'.

By including the expulsion of the Dutch in his demands, Vivero brought the war between Spain and Holland to Japan and forced Ieyasu to take sides. But Ieyasu avoided siding with either the Spanish or the Dutch by postponing his decision on the issue.

Be that as it may, there is some doubt as to the credibility of Vivero's statement regarding Ieyasu's promise to protect the priests. According to other sources of the time, Ieyasu consistently refused to accept such demands. This is clear from the letter Ieyasu sent to King Philip immediately after his meeting with Vivero, in which Ieyasu asks only for the opening of trade.

Vivero continued to negotiate, even postponing his return, but this did not lead to the expulsion of the Dutch, as he had hoped it would. Finally, on 1 August 1610, Vivero set sail from Uraga for New Spain. For this purpose, Ieyasu gave him the second ship Adams had built. In the letter to his 'unknown friends and countrymen', Adams proudly stated that Ieyasu had lent the governor of Manila the ship he had built, named the *San Buena Ventura*, to sail to Acapulco.

Diplomatic Manoeuvres

When Adams met Puyck near Ushimado, Puyck had asked him to maintain good relations with Specx, the head of the Dutch trading post in Hirado. For the next two years, however, Adams received no news from Specx. The Dutch didn't send any ships to Japan the following year, in violation of their promises. But there was a good reason for this. Don Juan de Silva, the governor of the Philippines who had succeeded Vivero, was attempting a military expedition to wipe out the Dutch from the Moluccas, overrunning several Dutch strongholds. To counter this attack, the Dutch had to gather all their ships in the region.

Finally, in July 1611, a small ship, the *Brack*, arrived from Patani. Upon its arrival, Specx decided to go to Sunpu and Edo. He wanted to pay his respects to Ieyasu and apologize for the lack of ships the previous year. On 5 July, Specx wrote to Adams, asking him to wait for the Dutch at Sunpu and not to come to Hirado in search of them. He didn't want to miss Adams on his way, as Puyck had done two years before. He entrusted the letter to a courier and urged him to reach Adams as soon as possible.

Specx was eager for Adams's help as he intended to petition Ieyasu for better trade terms. As mentioned above, the governor of Nagasaki had imposed various trade restrictions on the Portuguese and was keeping close watch. The Dutch wanted the privilege of buying and selling goods in Japan with complete freedom, without interference from the Nagasaki magistrates, but this was no easy task. Specx didn't have the confidence to conduct these difficult negotiations alone; he needed Adams's help to achieve his goal. In his diary of the court journey, Specx wrote:

> This Mr Adams is esteemed by Ieyasu as a prince or potentate because of his learning and sincerity. He is entitled to converse directly and intimately with his highness [Ieyasu]. This is a great help to us, as few people are allowed to do this.

Specx's party left Hirado on 17 July. When they arrived in Kyoto on 7 August, they discovered that the letter they had sent to Adams by courier had been held up by various obstacles. Specx wrote a new letter and entrusted it to another courier. This second letter did find Adams. He guessed that the Dutch would be near Sunpu, and against Specx's wishes, he went out to meet them. This time they didn't miss each other. On 15 August, he met Specx and his party in the town of Mariko, where Adams gave Specx a detailed account of the arrival of the Spaniards and Portuguese.

As Pessoa's carrack had been sunk the previous year, no Portuguese ships sailed to Japan in 1610. However, the following year, a small Portuguese ship arrived in Satsuma. It was hastily fitted out in Macao for the sole purpose of carrying an envoy to Japan. The Portuguese chose Satsuma because they thought they would be more welcome there than in Nagasaki. They were unsure how they would be treated by the governor of Nagasaki after the incident.

The Portuguese left Satsuma for Osaka on two Japanese ships provided by an official of the Satsuma clan. From Osaka they travelled by land. The envoy made the journey in great style, playing shawms and trumpets along the way. Upon his arrival in Sunpu, the ambassador, Dom Nuño de Sotomayor, presented his case orally to Honda Masazumi and then submitted it in writing. The envoy also had an audience with Ieyasu. When they arrived at the castle, they came in a splendid procession, all dressed in velvet with gold chains around their necks. Ieyasu accepted their lavish gifts, but with little respect or kindness. He said not a word to the ambassador. After the Portuguese had handed over the gifts, they were told to leave at once.

Ieyasu did not like the ambassador's pleas. Sotomayor tried to justify Pessoa's actions in Macao. Many Japanese had been killed, but it was not Pessoa's fault, he argued. It was the Japanese who were to blame, so there was no need to sink the carrack. He even demanded payment for the damage, which amounted to millions of ducats. The Portuguese claimed that the governor of Nagasaki was the cause of the problem because he had not accurately informed Ieyasu about the matter. They gave all the gory details of the governor's misdeeds and wiles, and made many complaints against him.

In response, Ieyasu, through Masazumi, pointed out the obstinacy and improper behaviour of the ship's crew. In particular, the captain's refusal to appear before him to defend himself was a sure sign that he was the one to blame. Failure to appear was against the law in every country, not just Japan, and there was no excuse for it. Therefore, the disaster was self-inflicted, Ieyasu concluded. Having received this reply, the Portuguese envoy went to Edo to meet the shogun, Hidetada. Their prospects were bleak, to say the least.

Sebastián Vizcaíno,
after an engraving
from the 17th century.

The Spanish didn't sit idly by either. On 10 June, a ship carrying Sebastián Vizcaíno, ambassador of the viceroy of New Spain, arrived at the port of Uraga, near the Bay of Edo. Vizcaíno came to express his gratitude for the help Ieyasu had given Vivero when he had washed ashore in Japan two years earlier. He met Hidetada at Edo Castle on 22 June and Ieyasu at Sunpu Castle on 5 July. This was his first mistake.

Ieyasu was not pleased that the Spanish ambassador visited his son first and not himself. Nor was he happy with the way Vizcaíno arrived at Sunpu. The Spanish ambassador came with about forty musketeers, carrying a flag with the crest of the king of Spain. On their way to the castle, they sounded muskets and trumpets. Vizcaíno was told that he would have to leave them behind if he wanted to enter the castle. Indeed, it was not Japanese custom to go to the castle armed when having an audience with the lord. But

Vizcaíno, eager to show the greatness of the king of Spain, would not listen. He took his soldiers and came to the front of the castle with the king's flag. To the Japanese, Vizcaíno's behaviour seemed rude and arrogant. The flags, muskets and trumpets probably reminded them of an army marching into battle. The Spaniards passed through the gate with much ceremony, but only Vizcaíno and his Franciscan interpreter were allowed to enter the palace.

At the audience, Vizcaíno presented the gifts of the viceroy of New Spain and made four demands. First, permission to build ships in Japan; second, permission for Spanish navigators to enter all Japanese coasts and ports; third, the expulsion of the Dutch from Japan; and fourth, free trade without supervision. Of these, the expulsion of the Dutch was Vizcaíno's most important task. He added that he hoped the king of Spain would be allowed to send warships to destroy the Dutch ships anchored in Japanese harbours.

Ieyasu, who was in a bad mood because of Vizcaíno's behaviour, said very little to him. But he agreed to all the demands

Eastern gate and adjoining turret of Sunpu Castle, rebuilt in 1989–96.

except the expulsion of the Dutch. Ieyasu jokingly replied that 'his country was free and open to all foreign nations. In this respect he would favour the Dutch as much as any other.' He added, 'It is no concern of his if a Dutch prince is at war with another country. Let that be settled between the warring nations.' With this answer, Vizcaíno returned to Uraga, where his ship was anchored.

All of this information can be found in Specx's diary. He wrote down everything that Adams told him, and Adams knew all this because he had been present at the audience. When, during the same audience, Adams asked Vizcaíno about the truce between Spain and Holland, Vizcaíno claimed to know nothing about it. When Adams refuted this and told him that he should know in front of Ieyasu, Vizcaíno responded with a fierce rebuttal. This argument between the two must have increased Ieyasu's distrust of the Spaniards.

With this detailed report from Adams on the Portuguese and Spanish envoys, Specx and his party continued their journey, arriving in Sunpu on 15 August. It was already dark, but Adams paid a visit to Honda Masazumi and Gotō Shōzaburō, two of Ieyasu's closest aides. Masazumi had served Ieyasu since childhood, along with his father Masanobu. Shōzaburō was the master of the mint, entrusted with important tasks ranging from the shogunate's finances to international trade. Adams informed both of Specx's arrival and asked for an audience with Ieyasu at the earliest opportunity. Masazumi replied that Ieyasu would be pleased by their arrival. The next day, Adams brought Specx to the castle twice, but the audience did not take place as Ieyasu was busy checking accounts.

On the morning of 17 August, Adams took Specx to the residence of Gotō Shōzaburō. As was customary in Japan, he presented Shōzaburō with some gifts. Shōzaburō accepted them with gratitude and promised Specx that he would grant him an audience with Ieyasu the same day. The subject then turned to the alleged piracy of the Dutch. Vizcaíno visited Shōzaburō's house before the Dutch arrived and argued that the Dutch were pirates. Vizcaíno's arguments were so convincing that Shōzaburō suspected he was telling the truth. During Adams's visit the previous day, Shōzaburō had suggested to Adams that 'since the Portuguese and Spaniards had come to Japan this year, the Dutch seem to have come to Japan to capture their ships. Didn't the Dutch come without goods, both last time and this time?' Adams reacted vehemently to these accusations. 'The Dutch are not thieves, but merchants,' he declared, adding:

> The Dutch visit Japan to trade with honesty and sincerity, not to seize Portuguese or Spanish ships. At the request of the king of Spain, the Dutch have concluded a twelve-year truce with Spain, whereby they will not harm each other wherever they may be.

Adams's strong assurances convinced Shōzaburō. He told Adams that he was glad to know. However, the cautious Shōzaburō took advantage of Specx's visit to ask him if everything Adams had said was really true. Specx took the time to explain to him the heart of the matter. Shōzaburō was glad to hear of the truce, for he hoped that the foreign nations coming to Japan would be able to concentrate on trade without engaging in hostilities with each other.

When Adams and Specx heard Masazumi had returned from the castle, they bade farewell to Shōzaburō and went straight to Masazumi's residence. He gave them a cordial welcome, and, as he had done on his visit to Shōzaburō, Specx presented him with several gifts. Like Shōzaburō, Masazumi accepted them. Then, out of the blue, he asked Specx the purpose of the Dutchman's visit to Ieyasu. Specx replied that he had come to apologize to Ieyasu for not sending ships the previous year and to explain the situation in

Asia. Satisfied with this answer, Masazumi promised to tell Ieyasu so and asked if he had anything else to petition Ieyasu for. This conversation suggests that Adams had discussed the matter with Masazumi beforehand. Here Specx brought up the subject of free trade. He wanted a licence to buy and sell goods in Japan with complete freedom – that is, without interference from the Nagasaki magistrate. Adams's preliminary negotiations seemed to have worked, and Masazumi replied to Specx that the petition made sense. He assured them that it would not be rejected, and he would see that everything was settled before they returned from Edo.

After a brief chat about the situation in Holland, they parted company. Masazumi saw the Dutch off at the gate. But then he called Adams back and told him he wanted to return the gifts. Fearing that this would spoil the good mood, Adams pleaded with him to take them not as gifts, but as Dutch souvenirs. Masazumi pondered for a moment and then, sensing Adams's intentions, said, 'I will accept them contrary to custom, so that the Dutch will not mistrust my feelings towards them.' He then called the Dutch back in to tell them so. In this way, Adams skilfully created a favourable environment for the Dutch at court.

Around noon, Specx was summoned by Masazumi. Adams took him to the castle. There, Specx had an audience with Ieyasu and presented him with gifts. These gifts were placed on low tables, according to Japanese custom. Ieyasu asked about the situation in Asia and about various products such as camphor, agarwood and aloeswood. Satisfied with Specx's answers, he gave the Dutch permission to leave. Masazumi and Shōzaburō stepped forward and escorted Specx out of the room. They congratulated him and expressed their surprise that he had been allowed to speak so intimately with Ieyasu.

Adams was then summoned back inside. When he came in, he saw Ieyasu inspecting Specx's gifts of woollen cloth, moiré silk, velvet and guns. He told Adams that he hoped the Dutch would return and import many rare and beautiful products. Adams nodded at these words and said that the first ships would bring many exquisite goods. At this, Ieyasu said, 'Yes, yes, I know very well that the Dutch are skilled in both crafts and warfare.'

After the audience, Specx had his petition for free trade written and translated into Japanese, and on 18 August he handed it to Masazumi through Adams. The next day they left Sunpu for Edo.

Discord with the Spanish Ambassador

They arrived in Edo three days later. Adams escorted Specx to his residence in Nihonbashi and went to inform Honda Masanobu, Hidetada's chief aide and Masazumi's father, of the arrival of the Dutch. The next morning, Adams took the Dutch to Masanobu's residence. Despite his illness, Masanobu gave them a warm welcome. They discussed world affairs and the war between Holland and Spain. Masanobu expressed his amazement that the small Dutch nation had held out for so long against the mighty Spanish Empire. This shows that he was well informed about the political situation in the world. After about thirty minutes, Masanobu saw them out, although his illness and old age made it difficult for him to walk. Specx and his party returned to Adams's house, where they stayed for a while.

At about two o'clock, one of Masanobu's retainers arrived at Adams's residence to inform him that they had been summoned to the castle. Adams then escorted Specx to Edo Castle, where they were brought before Hidetada. Specx presented Hidetada with gifts selected according to Adams's advice. After the audience, Adams took the Dutch to his residence and went to Masanobu to thank him for his efforts. Masanobu told him the details of the Spanish ambassador's audience with Hidetada. On his return Adams told Specx about it.

After a short stay of only three days, Adams and his party boarded a ship prepared by Masanobu for Uraga on 25 August. They arrived in Uraga on the evening of the same day and stayed at Adams's house (Adams had a residence in Uraga as well as in Edo, Sunpu and Hemi). By chance, Vizcaíno was also staying in Uraga; when the Spanish ambassador heard of the arrival of the Dutch, he sent two or three men to Adams's house to welcome them. They behaved with great respect and social courtesy, but the Dutch saw through the pretence. They responded with superficial politeness.

Now that he knew that Vizcaíno was staying in Uraga, Adams could not contain his anger. During his stay in Sunpu, Vizcaíno had made a series of false accusations against the Dutch to Ieyasu, Shōzaburō and others. The Dutch were 'scoundrels, traitors to the king of Spain and pirates'. This situation must have brought back to Adams's mind memories of the slander he had received from the Jesuits when he drifted ashore in Japan, fearing for his life.

He couldn't bear it any longer. Adams ran out of the house and went straight to Vizcaíno's lodgings. As soon as he arrived, he protested to the ambassador. He asked him why he spoke of the Dutch as if they were 'pirates and a people that could only do harm'. Vizcaíno was not at all intimidated by Adams's words and added fuel to the fire by saying: 'I have indeed said this to the Japanese sovereign, and yet it was not enough.' He told Adams: 'If the Dutch want, I will give them a satisfactory account of who they are, face to face.' Disgusted, Adams had nothing more to say and walked away. He vowed that under no circumstances would he act as an intermediary for the Spanish and Portuguese in their efforts to obtain free trade in Japan.

Adams and his Dutch friends left Uraga in the morning of 27 August, stopping at Kamakura at midday and arriving at Ōiso in the evening, where they spent the night. They set out again at dawn on the following day, arriving at Yoshiwara in the evening.

Two days later, they mounted their horses again and reached Sunpu in the afternoon. Adams went directly to Masazumi's residence to report the arrival of the Dutch. There he discovered that although a red seal pass had been arranged, the licence for free trade without interference requested by Specx had not been prepared.

As far as Masazumi was concerned, the licence was not worth the trouble of putting it down on paper; he probably wanted to leave it ambiguous. But Specx definitely wanted it in writing, so Adams spent the next few days negotiating. His persistence paid off, and he got permission from Masazumi to go to the castle. He arrived there around noon on 2 September with Specx's petition and informed Ieyasu of the Dutch request. Convinced, Ieyasu had a licence drawn up, stamped and handed to Adams. Thanks to these efforts, the negotiations for free trade at Sunpu ended in a great success for the Dutch.

But there was one thing that worried Adams: when Vizcaíno visited Sunpu, he received a red seal pass from Ieyasu authorizing him to survey Edo Bay. Adams told Ieyasu that this survey was highly suspicious. 'The only reason for the Spaniards to survey Edo Bay was to prepare for an invasion by a large fleet. England would never allow another country to survey her shores,' he said. Ieyasu was surprised but apologetic, saying that he would lose face if he refused now. He assured Adams that if the Spaniards invaded, he need not worry as he had plenty of men to defend himself. But Adams remembered the Spanish plan to invade England that he had witnessed in his youth. He told Ieyasu, 'The Spanish always send missionaries first to convert a large number of the country's people to Christianity, and then they conspire with the Christians to conquer the country and make it the property of the king of Spain.'

A few months later, a case of bribery between Okamoto Daihachi, a vassal of Honda Masazumi, and Arima Harunobu, the lord of Hinoe in Kyushu, came to light. Both were Christians. The execution of Daihachi and the *seppuku* of Harunobu settled the case. However, the interrogation revealed that there were many Christians living in Sunpu Castle; Adams's warning had come true. On 21 April 1612, the same day as the execution, Ieyasu issued a decree banning Christianity in the territories under his control. Churches were destroyed and priests exiled. Several Spanish and Portuguese writers of the time claimed that Adams was responsible for the oppression of the Christians.

Meanwhile, Vizcaíno set sail from Uraga in search of the legendary Islands of Gold and Silver, which he believed lay to the east of Japan. Vizcaíno tried to keep this mission secret from Ieyasu and Hidetada, but Adams had learned of the plan in Uraga from a Dutch sailor on Vizcaíno's ship and informed Ieyasu. In the end, Vizcaíno's expedition was fruitless, because the islands did not exist. To make matters worse, his ship was caught in a storm and wrecked during his search. Vizcaíno planned to build a new ship and return home, but he needed the help of the shogunate.

When Vizcaíno learned that Ieyasu was in Edo, he sought an audience with him to ask for his help. However, Ieyasu refused to meet him. Vizcaíno remained in Edo for five months, offering various gifts and petitions. On one occasion, he waited for Ieyasu on his way to hunt, enduring hardship and cold. Despite these efforts, he was never allowed to see Ieyasu again. The sale of the goods he had imported did not go well either.

Penniless, Vizcaíno left Japan aboard the *San Juan Bautista*. This ship was built by order of Date Masamune, a powerful warlord. Its purpose was to carry the 'Keichō envoy' to Mexico. From there, the envoy would travel to Europe to meet Pope Paul v in Rome. The purpose of this envoy is shrouded in mystery, but it was probably a final attempt to establish trade relations with Spain.

Working for the Dutch

After obtaining a free trade licence, Specx returned to Hirado, with Adams accompanying him. The party left Sunpu on 3 September and arrived in Kyoto five days later. Itakura Katsushige, the *shoshidai* (representative of the shogun in the capital), received them in audience. After a warm welcome, they left Kyoto early in the morning on 10 September, arriving at Fushimi around midday. From there they took a small boat down the river to Osaka, where they arrived the morning after.

At Osaka, they transferred to a small ship owned by the Dutch East India Company and sailed through the Seto Inland Sea. They reached Hirado at dawn on 19 September. They first visited the old and young lords of Hirado, presenting them with letters from Masazumi, Shōzaburō and Katsushige and reporting the results of their voyage. Because of the seasonal winds, the *Brack* had to set sail as soon as possible, and Specx was busy selling the cargo and fitting out the ship. Meanwhile, Adams enjoyed the company of the Dutch crew. In particular, he got to know Pieter Janssen, the *Brack*'s second pilot.

From this new friend, Adams learned something unexpected: English ships had been sailing to Asia for some time, and there had long been an English trading post at Bantam in Java. Specx had told Adams nothing of this. He also discovered that letters he had sent with the Dutch to his wife and friends in England had never reached their addressees. They were intercepted by the directors of the Dutch East India Company.

Nevertheless, Adams's wife and friends in England and Holland knew of his presence in Japan. They sent several letters, which also failed to reach Japan because of the interference of the Dutch East India Company. When a shocked Adams asked for an explanation, Specx must have been at a loss for an answer. This was nothing less than an act of betrayal against Adams, who had done so much for the Dutch. Specx tried to explain to him that, in accordance with the directors' policy of secrecy, the sending of letters was officially forbidden, but Adams was not convinced.

Adams immediately wrote two new letters, one to his wife in England and the other to his 'unknown friends and countrymen'. In both letters he recounted events from the time he sailed from Holland until 1611. The letter to his wife has not survived, but the first half was published in 1625 in Samuel Purchas's *Hakluytus Posthumus; or, Purchas His Pilgrimes*, a collection of travel journals. This suggests that the letter somehow reached England, although the second half of the letter was probably suppressed. A copy of the other letter, addressed to his 'unknown friends and countrymen', is also found in Purchas's book, so the two letters seem to have arrived in England together. It seems to have been addressed to members of the English trading post at Bantam. After an account of events from his departure from Holland until 1611, Adams gives a brief description of the Japanese people. He writes:

> The people of the land are good of nature, courteous out of measure, and valiant in wars; justice is severely executed upon the transgressor of the law without partiality; governed in great civilly, I mean not a land better governed in the world by civil policy.

This brief description of the nature of the Japanese gives us an idea of Adams's affinity with them. By this point in his life, Adams had integrated himself into Japanese society and enjoyed its benefits. His nostalgia for England was fading. Hoping they would reach his wife, children and friends, Adams gave the letters to Janssen just before the *Brack* left Japan. Janssen took Adams's letters with him and gave them to Augustine Spalding, a member of the English trading post at Bantam, who ensured their safe forwarding to London.

Although furious at the Dutch East India Company's intrusion into his private correspondence, Adams still wanted to assist the Dutch. He accepted Specx's request to help sell the goods imported by the *Brack* and brought them to Osaka in a small ship. He also sent timber from Osaka to Hirado to build the Dutch trading post. With the help of merchants in Osaka, Adams sold ivory, silk and woollen goods for the Dutch in Sakai and Osaka. But from his correspondence with Specx during this period, it seems that selling was not Adams's strong point. He was particularly uncomfortable with discounting. As sales were poor, Specx sent his assistant Mathias and Jan Cosyns, a former crew member of the *Liefde*, to Kyoto to take over sales.

Apart from sales, Adams supported the Dutch in every way. He seems to have been on friendly terms with various foreigners in Japan, including the Dutch, Italians, Portuguese and Spaniards. This tells us that Adams's resentment was not directed at all Spaniards or Portuguese. Using this network, he acted as an agent for Specx in the delivery of goods and letters. Adams also acted as an intermediary when Ieyasu purchased large quantities of iron sand from the Dutch, which was used to make Japanese swords.

In a letter to Adams dated 25 August 1612, Specx brought the happy news that a Dutch ship had arrived in Hirado. On board was Hendrik Brouwer, who was to replace Specx as head of the Dutch trading post at Hirado. Letters from Adams's wife and friends arrived on the same ship. Brouwer delivered the letters to Adams during his court journey to Sunpu and Edo. The letter from his wife was not written in reply to Adams's letter, since at that point it hadn't reached her. Rather, she wrote it on her own initiative after hearing that Adams was alive in Japan. The other letter was a reply to Adams's letter, which Janssen had handed to Spalding.

Brouwer went to Sunpu and Edo for audiences with Ieyasu and Hidetada, and Adams supported the Dutch to the best of his ability, as he had done the previous year. Ieyasu wanted the Dutch to move their trading post to Uraga, since it was close to Edo, so Adams took Brouwer there to inspect the harbour. Although Brouwer agreed that Uraga was a better anchorage than Hirado, he refused to relocate the trading post; they had already built one at Hirado, and moving it to another place would cost too much money. On this occasion, Adams provided Brouwer with a map of Japan. Brouwer sent this map to the governor of the Dutch East India Company, but it was subsequently lost. During the audience with Ieyasu, Brouwer handed over a letter from Prince Maurice and received a friendly reply from Ieyasu. In this way, relations between Japan and the United Provinces developed on friendly terms, but it is Adams who deserves the credit for creating this favourable environment.

5

The Coming of the English

Giving so admirable and affectionated commendatyons of
the Counterye as it is generally thought emongst us that he is a
naturalised Japanner.

Journal of JOHN SARIS, 29 July 1613

John Saris's first impression of William Adams was an under-standable one. Saris was the captain of the first English ship to arrive in Japan, in 1613, and Adams spoke so enthusiastically about Japan and its people that his newly arrived countrymen thought Adams himself had become Japanese. In fact, after living in the country for thirteen years, he would have looked a lot like a Japanese person, since he probably dressed like them.

A Letter to the English East India Company

In addition to the two letters Brouwer had given Adams at their meeting in Sunpu, Adams received two more. Pieter Janssen, who had carried Adams's letters to Bantam, arrived in Hirado a little later than Brouwer on the Dutch ship the *Hasewindt*. On the way to Hirado, the ship called at Patani, where the English handed Janssen two letters addressed to Adams. Janssen made sure that the letters were not opened before they were given to Adams.

One of the letters was from Adams's good friend John Stokley. The other was from Sir Thomas Smythe, the governor of the

English East India Company. In this letter, Smythe told Adams that he planned to send ships to Japan and establish a trading post there. On hearing this, Adams's heart was filled with hope. He went to Ieyasu and told him that the king of England would send an envoy and traders to Japan the following year. Ieyasu was delighted to hear this news. He was glad the English king showed such a friendly attitude towards his country and talked at length with Adams about trade.

After meeting with Ieyasu and Hidetada, Adams accompanied Brouwer to Hirado, where he wrote a letter to Spalding. In this letter, Adams explained the censorship by the Dutch East India Company and Janssen's efforts. He told how much Ieyasu was looking forward to the arrival of the English ships. 'There has not nor shall not be a nation more welcome,' he wrote to Spalding, and assured him that he had the power to secure a favourable trade agreement for the English because he was on such good terms with Ieyasu. Adams also gave Spalding a detailed account of trade and customs in Japan. He further mentioned that the Spanish and Portuguese had asked him to act as an intermediary with Ieyasu. They wanted to get the same free trade rights as the Dutch, but Adams refused: 'The Spaniards and Portuguese had been my bitter enemies to death, and now they must seek to me, an unworthy wretch, for the Spaniards so well as the Hollanders must have all their negotiations go through my hand.'

At the end of the letter, Adams recommended that if a ship came to Japan, it should sail to the eastern part of the country. By 'eastern part', Adams meant the harbour of Uraga near Edo, where the shogun lived. When the ship arrived near the coast, they were to ask for Adams. 'I am called in the Japanese tongue Angin Sama. By that name am I known all the sea coast along,' he added.

Adams wrote the letter to Spalding in Hirado on 12 January 1613. Since Janssen did not board the returning Dutch ship, but remained in Hirado, Adams had to entrust the letter to someone else. This person was Thomas Hill, a man Adams referred to as 'a good friend'. The name suggests he was English. He served on the Dutch ship as a pilot or sailor, and seems to have befriended Adams while they were both in Hirado. Hill delivered the letter to Spalding in Bantam.

Captain John Saris

While the Dutch established trading posts throughout Asia, the English focused their early presence in the region on Bantam. There they traded mainly for spices from the Moluccas. In the warm climate of Southeast Asia, however, there was no demand for English woollen goods. This led them to look for new markets to export to, and Japan was seen as having potential because of its cold winters. When the English fleet sailed from the Downs in 1611, the captain and chief commander of the fleet, John Saris, was ordered to buy spices in Bantam and sail to Japan. Once there, he was to make contact with William Adams. From these orders we can conclude that Adams was already known to be in Japan and in great favour with its ruler before Adams's letters reached England.

It was the first time Saris had been given command of a fleet. He was 32 years old at the time. In 1604, he joined the English East India Company and took part in the second voyage to Bantam and the Moluccas. When the fleet sailed back to England, Saris remained at the trading post in Bantam. In 1608, he was promoted to chief factor, but returned to England the following year. Back in England, the directors appointed Saris to be in command of the fleet that sailed for Asia in 1611. Saris's lengthy experience in Bantam and diligence in collecting useful information on the trade of the Far East made him a natural choice for the post.

It took Saris more than a year to reach Bantam, since he made a stopover at Mocha on the Red Sea. When he arrived on 24 October

1612, the Dutch controlled the spice trade; prices were high, and the English hopes of making a big profit were dashed. To find a way out of the situation, he called a meeting of his merchants on 28 October, where Adams's letter was read to them. This was most probably the letter to his 'unknown friends and countrymen', dated 23 October 1611, that Janssen gave to Augustine Spalding in Bantam. Trading in Japan, as recommended in Adams's letter, seemed promising: Japan was rich in silver, so by exchanging English woollen cloth for silver in Japan, a profitable trade could be established. Saris sent two of the three ships in his fleet home, loaded with 14,000 sacks of pepper, which he had bought at a premium. On 15 January 1613, Saris himself sailed for Japan in the remaining ship, the *Clove*.

After calling at the Moluccas, the *Clove* arrived at Hirado on 11 June 1613. Saris was welcomed by Matsura Shigenobu and his grandson Takanobu, the old and new lord of Hirado. On board the *Clove*, Saris entertained his guests and gave them a letter from the king of England. Shigenobu seemed pleased but said he would not open the letter until 'Ange' came to translate it for him. This event impressed upon Saris that Adams would be key in making his voyage to Japan a success. Saris promptly wrote a letter to Adams, and Shigenobu, believing Adams to be in Edo, sent a messenger to deliver it there.

All sorts of people came to visit the captain. Saris was surprised to see so many women visiting the ship. Among them were the lord's 'chief women'. They wore silk *kosode* with a sash around their waists. Their hair was black and long, tied in a neat knot at the top of their heads, an indication that they were in fact courtesans. Several high-ranking samurai also came to greet Saris. They too wore silk *kosode*, girded with a sash. Saris noticed the two swords at their sides, one long and one short. He found it strange that their heads were shaved to the crown, the rest of their hair tied in a knot behind. The hair was worn like this to make it easier to put on a helmet in battle. It also prevented the top of the head from becoming hot and damp. In times of peace, they left their heads bare, resulting in this peculiar fashion.

Saris could get along well with the old lord. Shigenobu visited him often, and they enjoyed chatting with each other. They did this through a Japanese interpreter that Saris had brought with him from Bantam, who understood Malay. Shigenobu would speak in Japanese and the interpreter would translate into Malay for Saris. Having spent many years in Bantam, Saris apparently knew enough Malay to keep the chat going.

The old lord of Hirado granted Saris a house ashore, where he awaited Adams's arrival. During this time, he learned of a song called 'Kurofune'. The lyrics described the capture of a Spanish ship by the English. As they sang, the Japanese acted like pirates with their swords at their sides, trying to frighten their children. Saris was surprised that the English had been known to the Japanese for so long that songs had been written about them. He found out that the song was inspired by the Jesuits, who had called Adams and his companions pirates when the *Liefde* drifted ashore. Three weeks passed and still no news of Adams. Worried, Saris wrote another letter and sent it with Shima, a retainer of the lord of Hirado. Shima was leaving for Osaka, and Saris asked him to deliver the letter to Adams if he met him on the way.

On 7 July, two Spaniards came to visit Saris. They said they knew Adams, and asked permission to board the ship, which Saris granted, although he suspected them of being spies. The Spaniards toured the ship and left. Saris was then informed that Adams was on good terms with the Spanish, the sworn enemies of the English. He became suspicious and questioned Adams's loyalty to his own country.

A few days later the Dutchman Melchior van Santvoort also came to visit. He had just returned from Siam (now Thailand) and brought Adams letters from Lucas Anthonysen, a Dutchman in the service of the English there, which he delivered to Saris. Van

Santvoort told Saris that he lived in Sakai, where he was married to a Japanese woman. Finding him a steady and understanding person, Saris suggested he take him to England, but Van Santvoort refused. He said that life in Japan was far more satisfying than in his own country. A few days later, Saris received a visit from another Dutchman. This time it was Lodensteijn, also from Siam. Like Van Santvoort, Lodensteijn entrusted Saris with a letter for Adams. The old lord joined them, but later told Saris that Lodensteijn was not to be trusted and that he was deeply in debt in Japan.

More than a month had passed and there was still no news of Adams. Shima returned from Osaka on 20 July. He brought the letter back that Saris had entrusted to him because he hadn't seen Adams. The long wait tried Saris's patience, but finally, on 29 July, Adams arrived in Hirado. The reason he took so long was that the messenger rushed to Edo while Adams stayed in Sunpu. Another messenger missed him on the way. Shigenobu wanted to banish them, but Saris entreated him for mercy. Adams, for his part, rushed to Hirado when he heard of the English ship's arrival.

Adams boarded the *Clove* and received a warm welcome by the crew. Saris, who was ashore, sent merchants Richard Cocks and Tempest Peacock to the ship to take Adams to the house where he was staying. The English treated Adams like a king, giving him a three-volley salute as he boarded the ship and another nine volleys as he landed. Saris paid his respects to Adams as best he could when he arrived at his house. After a brief chat, the subject turned to the course to be taken. Saris informed him that he had brought a letter from King James to Ieyasu. Adams advised him to deliver it as soon as possible.

After so many years, Saris expected Adams to be excited to meet his compatriots, but no such touching moments occurred. Instead, Adams couldn't stop talking about Japan. This made the English feel uncomfortable: Adams spoke of Japan with such affection that they thought he had become a 'naturalized Japanese', meaning that he had become more attached to Japan than to England.

The subject of trade was another disappointment. When told of the *Clove*'s cargo, Adams declared that no profit could be expected. The Dutch and Spanish had been importing woollen cloth in large quantities for some years, which had caused the price of this product to fall sharply. As for spices, they weren't used much in Japan and wouldn't sell well. The other goods were also unprofitable because of low market prices. Adams's comments put a damper on Saris's hopes. Nevertheless, Saris spared no effort to create a friendly atmosphere. He asked Adams to choose any room in the house and to tell the cook what he liked best. Yet, Adams entreated him to pardon him. He would stay for three or four days in a poor house in the town, he said, and then turned to leave.

This came as a complete surprise to Saris, who had waited so long for Adams's arrival. He urged him in vain to stay with him, as he wanted to discuss trade in Japan, but Adams said he would be with Saris when he wished to send for him. Until then, he would be at his poor house or at the Dutch trading post. And so, Adams took his leave. Several merchants offered to accompany him, but he refused. The English felt offended that Adams did not consider them worthy enough to accompany him; surely Adams must have been delighted to be reunited with his countrymen? But he valued his 'freedom' above all else. He had been away from home for fifteen years and had integrated himself into Japanese society; he could not pretend that all those years had never passed. Valuing the sincere bonds of friendship, Adams had no interest in superficial acts of respect. It seems that Saris's efforts to show formal respect at their first meeting did not have the desired result. Rather, they caused Adams to keep his distance.

Saris, not understanding such an attitude, kept trying, and invited Adams to dine on board the next day. Adams did indeed dine with Saris, but he did not stay long. Several Spaniards and Portuguese came from Nagasaki to visit him, and as soon as he had finished eating, Adams went to see them. This act gave the English the further impression that Adams valued people from other countries more than his own. But there was another reason for Adams's behaviour: he felt responsible for these Spaniards. They had come to Japan on Vizcaíno's ship but had deserted when Vizcaíno was in dire straits. Adams protected them and hid them in Nagasaki. When Adams asked him to take them to Bantam aboard the *Clove*, Saris refused because they were deserters. This further widened the gap between them. Still, Saris tried to keep his anger to a minimum and decided to give Adams an elaborate gift, which he thought might make him feel more affectionate towards his countrymen. 'For that no penny, no paternoster in this age,' Saris wrote in his journal. The English decided to give him several expensive cloths. Saris himself presented him with some fine clothes, a carpet and some books. But even these gifts had no effect on Adams's attitude. As before, Saris's attempts to win him over proved unsuccessful.

On 2 August, Adams was invited to the Dutch trading post. Saris became suspicious again. To find out what business Adams had with his Dutch rivals, he asked him to take Richard Cocks with him. After much pleading, Adams agreed. The English found out that Adams had been selling goods for the Dutch. The fact that Adams was on good terms with people from so many other countries puzzled the English, as we can see from Saris's journal and Cocks's letters. Having been in Japan for so long without meeting any of his fellow countrymen, it was only natural for Adams to develop close relationships with some foreigners. The English, however, perceived this attitude as a betrayal of his native country.

The Letter from King James

Saris wanted to prepare for the court journey as soon as possible. He persuaded Adams to stay at his house on 3 August to discuss the details of the journey. The time was well spent, and Adams gave Saris valuable advice on gifts for Ieyasu, Hidetada and the shogunate's senior officials, as well as on other matters.

On 7 August, Saris left for Sunpu on one of Shigenobu's ships. He was accompanied by ten Englishmen, a Japanese interpreter, a samurai with three guards, a Japanese spear-bearer, and Adams and his two servants, twenty men in all. They sailed through the Seto Inland Sea and arrived in Osaka on 27 August. From Osaka they travelled overland via Kyoto to Sunpu. They reached Sunpu on the morning of 6 September, and after showing the party to their lodgings, Adams went to Ieyasu's secretary and informed him of the arrival of the English. He was told that Saris was welcome and should have access to Ieyasu within a day or two.

The next day, they rested and prepared the gifts. On 8 September, only two days after their arrival, they were summoned. Adams took Saris to Sunpu Castle, where Gotō Shōzaburō and others welcomed them. But then an incident occurred. While waiting in the hall, Saris asked Adams to tell the secretary, Honda Masazumi, that he would deliver the king's letter to Ieyasu with his own hands. Stunned by this unexpected request, Adams went to Masazumi and told him. Surprised, Masazumi replied that it was not the custom of the country to deliver a letter to the lord in the hand of a stranger, but he proposed a compromise: Saris would hold the letter in his hand until they came into Ieyasu's presence. At that moment, Masazumi would take the letter from him and hand it to Ieyasu. When Adams informed Saris of this answer, the captain became angry. He told Adams he would return to his lodgings unless he could deliver the letter to Ieyasu himself. Adams went back to Masazumi and told him Saris's reply, which caused Masazumi to be annoyed that Adams had not properly informed Saris of Japanese customs. Adams was at a loss; he told Saris about Masazumi's answer, only to get a disgruntled reply.

Just as Adams wondered what would happen, Ieyasu appeared. The captain was brought before him. At that moment, Masazumi snatched the letter from Saris's hand and handed it to Ieyasu. That was the end of the matter, and Adams felt relieved. Ieyasu bade Saris a warm welcome after such a tiring journey and thanked him for bringing the letter from King James. He then asked if Saris intended to visit his son Hidetada in Edo. Saris replied that he did. Ieyasu said that orders should be given to provide Saris with men and horses for the journey. When he returned, his reply to the king of England would be ready. Satisfied with the audience, Saris took his leave and went back to his lodgings.

Meanwhile, Ieyasu summoned Adams and asked him to translate the letter from King James. Adams read the letter to Ieyasu and explained its contents. The letter itself has not survived, but there is a draft in the British Library. In it, King James explained that he had sent his subjects to Japan to solicit Ieyasu's friendship with the English and also to exchange such goods as might be most useful to each country. A Japanese translation can be found in the *Ikoku Nikki* (Diary of Foreign Relations). This manuscript was compiled by Ishin Sūden, the same author as the *Ikoku Goshuinchō* we saw in Chapter Four. The *Ikoku Nikki* contains Sūden's daily notes on foreign affairs. Among other things, he recorded that Adams had translated the contents of King James's letter into Japanese using kana. This is a Japanese phonetic alphabet derived from kanji (Chinese characters). Kanji was used for official documents, while kana tended to be used for private documents or as auxiliary characters. From this record we know that Adams could write Japanese in the phonetic alphabet, but not in kanji.

If we compare the original text with Adams's translation, we can see that the content is faithfully conveyed, but in a form that was easy for the Japanese to understand. For example, one sentence in the original text reads: 'We have encouraged our said subjects to undertake a voyage into your country, as well as to solicit your friendship and amity with us.' Adams's Japanese version can be translated as follows: 'I have sent Captain General John Saris and others as my envoys to pay our compliments to the Shogun Sama of Japan.' Adams transformed the abstract content of the original into a version acceptable to the Japanese ruler by making it concrete. This shows not only his linguistic skills, but his ability to transmit information between different cultures.

Ieyasu was in a good mood when he learned of King James's favourable attitude towards him and became open to the idea of creating diplomatic relations. He asked Adams several questions about the king of England, exploring the extent of his power, and ordered Adams to inform Saris that if he had any requests he should submit them to Masazumi, and they would be granted. Delighted, Adams went to the captain and informed him of Ieyasu's proposal. They drew up a petition of fourteen articles, which they presented to Masazumi the following day. After reviewing the request, Masazumi told Adams to simplify it, as the Japanese preferred brevity.

The next day, Adams submitted a simplified version of his request to Masazumi. The contents were acceptable to the secretary. Adams then went to the castle and handed the petition to Ieyasu. After some discussion, Ieyasu looked over the text. The simplified petition, consisting of seven articles, asked for almost the same privileges that had been granted to the Dutch two years earlier. These were that the English should be able to trade freely in Japan without interference, that their lives, ships and cargoes should be protected by Ieyasu and that they should be provided with food if necessary. After reading the demands, Ieyasu told Adams that he would grant them. As a result of Adams's efforts, a free trade agreement was signed between England and Japan. This was the second one Adams had brokered, the first being the free trade privileges won by the Dutch two years earlier.

The Northwest Passage

There was one clause in Saris's request that did not appear in the official document of privileges granted by Ieyasu, namely permission to travel to Ezo (now Hokkaido). This request was based not only on the prospect of trade in the area, but on plans to discover the Northwest Passage. The English had long sought a route to Asia along the northern coast of the North American continent. Adams thought that if they explored the route from Japan, they might find it. The Northwest Passage had long been Adams's favourite subject, so it is easy to imagine him telling Saris about it on the way to Sunpu. Saris must have thought it would do no harm to include an article on the topic in his request for permission to travel to Ezo.

The article caught the attention of Ieyasu. He asked Adams if the English could not find the Northwest Passage; Adams responded that the English had made many discoveries but had not yet found the passage. Ieyasu then asked if there was a way and if the distance was very short. Adams told him that he did not doubt it, and that the distance should be very short. He then showed Ieyasu the distance on a map of the world. When asked if the English knew of Ezo or Matsumae, the northern tip of Japan, Adams replied that he had never seen them on a Western map or globe.

Ieyasu next enquired if Saris's visit to Japan was to explore these northern regions; Adams told him he did not know. Ieyasu then asked him if he would like to go on such an expedition, and Adams was quick to say yes. He said that if the East India Company were to send or build a ship here, he would be most willing to take part in such an honourable enterprise. Sensing

Adams's enthusiasm, Ieyasu promised to write a letter of friend-ship to the people of Ezo, stating that his subjects in Matsumae lived in friendship with them. This conversation with Ieyasu gave Adams a new dream: hoping to embark on another great adven-ture, he wrote two letters outlining his plans to explore the Northwest Passage from Japan. One letter was addressed to the East India Company in London and the other to Thomas Best, an old friend of Adams's who was then stationed in Bantam as head of the English trading post.

In both letters, Adams argued strongly that England and Japan should work together to find the Northwest Passage. The Japanese would be of great help, Adams maintained, and letters of friendship from Ieyasu would be useful in places like Ezo. They could build ships in Japan, where shipwrights and timber were plentiful. They could also procure food in abundance for the voyage and employ the Japanese as crew. The English would only need to provide money, compasses and other navigational equipment, and men to command the Japanese crew.

In these letters, Adams's excitement is almost palpable. If the East India Company was willing to invest in the project, he wrote, 'by God's grace there will be great things found out in which to this time had not being heard of, and for my part [I] shall think myself a most happy man to be employed in such an honourable action.' This sentence reveals Adams's passion for adventure. The prospect of another achievement excited him. But this time, in contrast to the failure of the Van der Haegen fleet, he was going to prepare for the venture with great care. He felt that with the experience he had gained, he could achieve what others had failed to. And if he succeeded, England and Japan would be linked by a new, closer route.

On 12 October 1614, a year after Adams had written these two letters, the letter to Best was read to the directors of the East India Company in London. However, the records show that little attention was paid to Adams's plans. Since the route via the Cape of Good Hope was safe, the company was not interested in risking its money in the search for a new and unknown course. Meanwhile, in Japan, the great battle of Osaka was taking up all of Ieyasu's time and energy. As a result of these factors, Adams's dream of exploring the Northwest Passage fell by the wayside, never to be realized.

Conflict

The arrival of the English renewed Adams's desire to go back to his native land and be reunited with his wife and children. He wanted to be free to leave the country. After the success of Saris's audience, he asked his friends Masazumi and Shōzaburō to help him obtain Ieyasu's permission to return home, but both refused. They feared angering Ieyasu, as had happened on previous occasions.

With no one on his side, Adams decided to try it once more on his own. When they discussed world affairs and other matters, he found Ieyasu in a good mood. Not wanting to miss the opportunity, Adams plucked up courage. He took the red seal that granted him the estate in Hemi and placed it respectfully before Ieyasu. He then thanked him for his favour and love. A surprised Ieyasu asked him if he wished to go back to his country. 'Most desirous,' Adams answered. Ieyasu replied that if he were to detain him, he should do him wrong, for Adams had served him well. In all friendship, he gave Adams leave to decide whether to stay or go. Joyfully, Adams left, having thus won his freedom.

Having obtained the privilege of free trade from Ieyasu, Saris and Adams then proceeded to Edo, where Shogun Hidetada resided. They arrived in Edo on 14 September, and three days later they presented the gifts to Hidetada. On 21 September, Adams took Saris by ship to Uraga. He wanted him to inspect Uraga as a possible site for a trading post. Adams had recommended the harbour to the Dutch the previous year, but his efforts had been unsuccessful. Persuaded by Adams, Saris wrote in his journal that Uraga was a much better harbour than Hirado: the sea passage there seemed safe, and most importantly, Uraga was close to Edo.

While in Uraga, Adams showed Saris some artefacts made in Kyoto. These had been entrusted to him by the Spanish, and he wanted to sell them to the East India Company. Once again, Saris must have been disturbed by Adams's close contact with their 'enemies', but being a man of business, he was open to negotiation. However, just as he had done when selling goods for the Dutch, Adams would not lower the price. Nevertheless, he managed to sell a few pieces of lacquerware and eight folding screens. Saris probably accepted them out of courtesy. They stayed at Adams's house for three days. During his stay, Adams's Japanese wife, sister-in-law and mother-in-law treated Saris with great hospitality. As a token of his gratitude, he presented them with several gifts.

On their way back to Hirado, they stopped once more at Sunpu, where they found a red seal pass from Ieyasu and his reply to King James. In the letter, Ieyasu expressed his gratitude for the letters and gifts sent to him. He welcomed the English and promised to assist them in the future. The letter was written in Chinese by Sūden. Chinese was the language used for diplomatic documents in East Asia. Adams, who could not read Chinese kanji, got the help of a Japanese to translate it into English.

Thanks to Adams's efforts, Saris's court journey proved to be a great success. Besides, they achieved their audience with Ieyasu and Hidetada with unusual speed. Normally, Japanese lords showed their esteem for their guests by the length of time they let them wait for an audience. The sooner the audience was granted, the more highly the guest was regarded. On the other hand, the longer the lord made his guest wait, the less respect he showed. This was just one way of impressing guests with the power of the lord. When Saris met Ieyasu, it was in the assembly hall of Sunpu Castle, where all guests were received. Like the other palaces of the Tokugawa, the hall had gilded walls with magnificent paintings to impress. The guests sat with their legs crossed on tatami mats (a flooring material of a standard size of approximately 91 × 182 centimetres, consisting of straw which has been threaded through and hardened, with a surface of woven rush grass as the weft and a strip of cloth sewn around the edge), which were arranged in rows with the long side facing the inner part of the hall where the lord sat. The status of the guest determined how many rows of tatami mats away from the lord he was allowed to sit. The lord himself sat on a raised platform; on it, one or two tatami were stacked on top of each other to give the lord an even higher place to sit. The higher they sat, the more power they displayed. With Saris and other foreign envoys, Ieyasu went one step further. He would sit on a chair placed on the raised platform, placing himself even higher above the guests.

This was the way guests were treated, and everyone knew where they stood in the lord's esteem. The English got their audience so quickly because Ieyasu expected much from English trade. Saris owed this success to Adams; he knew this only too well. Even if there were doubts about Adams's patriotic feelings, all went smoothly, and the success of the mission eased the conflict between the two. They returned to Hirado together in good spirits, stopping in Kyoto to collect five pairs of large folding screens with paintings that Ieyasu had presented to King James.

On 6 November, at about ten o'clock in the morning, they arrived in Hirado. Much had happened in their absence. Cocks, who had been left in charge, had a hard time dealing with the rough English sailors. Every day they came ashore without permission and ran amok. Sometimes they escalated to the point of attacking the Japanese and fighting among themselves, causing injuries. Shortly after his arrival, Saris received a visit from the old and young lords of the domain, who warned him that the drawing of swords was punishable by death.

But this was not the only problem. Seven sailors had escaped in a small boat and were hiding in Nagasaki. At Saris's request, Adams set off to bring them back. There he was told by his friends that the English fugitives had already sailed to Manila and Macao on Spanish and Portuguese ships. Adams returned to Hirado without the sailors.

While Adams was away, Cocks complained to Saris about one of Adams's Japanese servants. This servant had a Christian name, Miguel, so it is safe to assume that he had been baptized. When Adams and his men left for Sunpu, Miguel remained in Hirado, acting as interpreter and caterer for the English. Cocks complained that Miguel was pocketing exorbitant fees for his services. Saris called for Adams. In the presence of Cocks, he told him of his servant's 'dishonest and villainous conduct'. Although the English trusted him because he was Adams's servant, he had betrayed that trust and deceived them. Saris wrote in his journal that he spoke to Adams about this in a 'friendly manner', but his actual words expressed disdain for the servant in question. Since Miguel was not in the service of the East India Company, it would be natural for him to charge for his services. Saris's criticism therefore seems unfounded.

Adams took it very badly that his servant should be thought of in this way. He argued bitterly with Saris. It was with great difficulty that Cocks managed to separate the two men. The mutual distrust that had existed between them came to the surface again, and they did not talk to each other for some time. Saris ordered Cocks not to allow Adams's servants to buy any more provisions. The situation worsened the next day when Cocks tried to repay Adams the money he had advanced during the court trip and for the goods Saris had bought from him in Uraga. Adams did not take kindly to being paid in Japanese silver coins rather than

Spanish reals. The money changers charged a commission of 5 per cent for exchanging Japanese silver for reals. But Saris considered Adams's request of being paid in reals unreasonable, since the lord of Hirado and the Dutch accepted Japanese silver without any problem.

While the relationship between the two men continued to deteriorate, Shigenobu entertained Saris with courtesans. Judging from Saris's journal, they got on well. On 26 November, Saris gathered his merchants and decided to set up a trading post in Hirado. His relationship with the lord of Hirado may have had a significant influence on this decision, which fell far short of Adams's hopes. Locating the trading post in Uraga, so close to Edo, would allow them to deal directly with the shogunate. As Ieyasu encouraged trade in Uraga, they could expect favourable treatment there. Access to the cities of Edo and Osaka was convenient, making it easy to sell goods. By choosing Uraga, the English would have a great advantage over the Dutch and Portuguese. Moreover, they would not be bothered by the lord of Hirado or the governor of Nagasaki. Best of all, Uraga was close to Adams's estate. Uraga was indeed the most sensible choice. On the other hand, the route to Uraga was long and dangerous because of the strong currents and could have delayed the English ships. From a navigator's point of view, therefore, Saris's decision was not entirely unreasonable.

The choice of Hirado as the location for the trading post was tantamount to ignoring Adams's advice. Although the decision was of vital importance to the company, Saris probably allowed his personal antipathy towards Adams and his preference for Shigenobu to prevail. Philip Rogers, who published one of the first biographies of Adams in 1956, stated that 'in rejecting Adams's advice Saris doomed the English trading project in Japan from the beginning.' With this remark, he hit the nail on the head. In Hirado, far from Edo, the English were helpless in

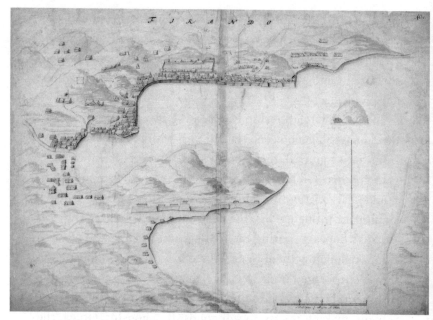

View of Hirado, 1621, drawn by a servant of the Dutch East India Company.

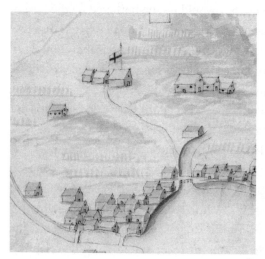

English trading post,
detail of *View of Hirado*.

the face of competition from the Dutch, who were already well established there.

Before deciding on the location of the trading post, Saris had summoned Adams. In the presence of Cocks and several other merchants, he asked Adams if he wanted to return home with him or stay in the country. Adams replied that he wanted to go home. But when asked if he would now return with him, Adams refused. He said that although he had served Ieyasu and received an estate, he had little money in his possession. Now that he was free, he wanted to save some before returning home. However, in a letter to the East India Company in London, Adams gave the real reason for his refusal. He wrote that he would not go with Saris because of 'diverse injuries' inflicted on him. For Adams, who had served the English so well, Saris's attitude was quite unexpected. Adams couldn't imagine making the long journey home with such a rude person.

Yet, there seems to have been some truth in the lack of money. As a retainer of Ieyasu, his income consisted mainly of rice, not cash. If he returned home, he would not have much to bring with him. At the very least, he would have to raise some money before he could leave. Moreover, he had lived in Japan for thirteen years and had a wife and children there. Even if he made up his mind to give all that up to go back home, he would have needed some time to prepare both financially and emotionally. It seems that it was more important for him to be free to return home than to actually do so. This strong commitment to freedom is evident in all the writings by and about Adams. Besides, a ship was expected every year, so there was no need to hurry.

The Contract

On learning of his intention to remain in Japan, Saris turned to Adams and asked him if he wished to work for the East India Company. Whatever their differences, he was well aware of the latter's influence at court, and hiring him would be in the best interests of the trading post. As for Adams, he needed the money, and earning a salary was more than he could hope for. So, he said yes.

Saris asked him on what terms. He brought up the matter of the £20 the Company had lent to Adams's wife in England. Mary, aware of Adams's presence in Japan and his connection with the East India Company, had borrowed the money when she was in need. Saris offered to forgive this debt in return for service to the Company. Adams expressed his gratitude but promised to pay the principal and interest himself. According to the account book of the Hirado trading post, he paid the debt soon after the departure of the *Clove*.

No longer able to use Mary's debt as a bargaining chip, Saris moved on to negotiating his salary. He asked Adams how much he wanted to be paid per year. When Adams said he wanted to be paid monthly rather than annually, Saris replied that the Company only paid annually, but Adams insisted otherwise. There were several reasons why Adams insisted on a monthly salary. With an annual one, he would not be paid for at least a year after he was hired, so it would be a long time before he had any cash in his hands. He also wasn't sure if he would get any money at all. If he received his salary on a monthly basis, he would have something real in his pocket sooner.

Looking for a clue to keep Adams interested, Saris asked what he wanted per month. Adams asked for £12 a month, saying that the Dutch had given him £15 when they employed him. On hearing Adams's terms, Saris asked Adams to leave the room and wait a moment. Adams was called back a short time later. Saris now offered him a salary of £80 a year, but Adams again refused. He had mixed feelings. On the one hand he felt the salary was too low for him, but at the same time he realized that it would be difficult for the company to make a profit in Japan that would justify such a high salary, so he was reluctant to accept Saris's offer. Above all, he did not want to lose his freedom. This is what Adams wrote to the East India Company in London, and it seems to express Adams's true feelings on the matter.

The supply of Chinese silk was crucial to making a profit in the trade with Japan. But the English had no access to the Chinese market, so they had to bring other products. Saris wanted to promote the sale of less profitable woollen cloth, but this was an area where the English faced stiff competition from the Dutch. Adams predicted that the company would not be able to make a significant profit in Japan with such a policy. He did not like the idea of being paid a large salary when his advice was ignored at every turn. Instead, he preferred to be free to share in the profits of Dutch or Spanish trade. They, at least, respected his advice. Yet he also felt it was his duty to help his fellow countrymen.

Saris failed to grasp Adams's mixed feelings. He interpreted Adams's hesitation as an act of bargaining, which was of course a factor, but not the main one. Saris offered Adams a salary of £80 a year, plus the £20 of his wife's debt, which he would waive. Adams flatly refused the offer. The two men were at loggerheads and agreed to take their time. After promising to give a resolute answer the next day, Adams left.

The next morning, Saris sent for Adams again and asked him about his decision. But Adams still hadn't made up his mind. At this point, Saris lost his patience and accused Adams of trying to extract the highest possible salary from the Company. Adams strongly denied this. He told Saris he hesitated because he didn't think he could make much profit for the Company under the present circumstances. But Saris didn't give up; he offered Adams a salary of £100 a year. Feeling that he could not refuse any longer, Adams relented and accepted the deal.

They agreed that Adams would be employed until a reply came from the East India Company to his proposal to explore the Northwest Passage. It would take a year for the *Clove* to travel to England and another year for a reply to be received, so the employment would last at least two years. According to the East India Company's rules, private trading was not allowed, and wages were not supposed to be paid until after two years. As this was too far in the future, Saris offered to lend him £20 to buy clothes and other necessities, which Adams accepted.

Two accounts of these negotiations have come down to us. The first is the contract itself between Adams and the East India Company, signed in Hirado on 24 November 1613. It records the details of the negotiations, but does not reveal the reasons for Adams's hesitation. The contract alone gives the impression that Adams negotiated skilfully to obtain the highest possible salary. This aspect has been emphasized in previous studies. The other evidence comes from two letters that Adams wrote, one to the East India Company and the other to Thomas Best. In these two letters, Adams explained his concerns about not wanting to be a burden on the company with his high salary, while at the same time wanting to be paid as much as the Dutch were paying him. He stated that these concerns were at the root of his difficulty in agreeing to the terms of his contract.

After signing the contract, Saris set up a trading post in Hirado, staffed by eight Englishmen, including Adams, and three Japanese interpreters. He appointed Cocks to head the trading post. Cocks, who came from a wealthy family, was already 49 years old, almost the same age as Adams. Before joining the East India Company, Cocks lived in Bayonne, a French town near the Spanish border, where he traded in woollen cloth and gathered information on developments in Spain. His knowledge of the cloth trade and the Spanish language led to his employment by the company. He sailed to Asia with Saris's fleet. It is difficult to say whether Cocks was the right man for the job. He seemed a friendly man and got on well with everyone, even Saris. But because of this soft character, he was not up to the task of controlling the rough sailors of the English ships calling at Hirado, or of competing with the Dutch.

Thus it looks as though Saris did not have a good eye for people. He had a very low opinion of Adams in particular. In a 'remembrance' he gave to Cocks before he left Japan, he warned him not to trust Adams. Adams was 'only fitting to be master of a junk and to be used as a linguist at court', Saris wrote – and even then, he was a man to watch out for. He was more affected to the Dutch and Spaniards than to his own countrymen. Nor should they trust him with their money, 'for his wish was but to have the Company bear his charges to his wife.' Yet, the contents of Saris's journal and Adams's letters do not support this assessment. It was through Adams's efforts that the English were able to obtain the most favourable terms of trade in Japan of any nation. Before signing the contract with the Company, Adams accompanied Saris to court, advised him on trade matters and obtained the trade privileges for him, all on a voluntary basis. Saris's perception of Adams deviated greatly from reality.

His view was also different from that of the Dutch. They were very disappointed that Adams was now working for the English. As Adams testified in his letters, the Dutch paid him a salary while he worked for them in 1611–12, and the Dutch East India Company also sent money to his wife in England. In a letter dated 26 October 1615, Gerard Reynst, the governor-general of the Dutch East India Company, commented to the 'Gentlemen XVII' or board of directors of the Dutch East India Company on Adams's contract with the English. He wrote that Adams had shown the Dutch much help and friendship in Japan and hoped that he would continue to do so. For his services, the Dutch East India Company had made payments to Mary Hyn, Adams's English wife. Perhaps this is why Adams had so little money with him in Japan. The Dutch paid at least part of his salary to his wife. In any case, Reynst feared that Dutch trade would be badly damaged if Adams were to divert his efforts to the English in the future. It is clear from this account that, unlike Saris, the Dutch had a high regard for Adams's abilities.

Saris arrived in Plymouth on 27 September 1614. There it was discovered that he had been trading privately, which was forbidden. The amount of spices he had bought for himself exceeded the amount he had brought back for the East India Company. Several crew members complained that they had been mistreated by their captain, and there were rumours of certain indecent books and pictures that Saris had brought back from Japan. This caused an uproar; the governor procured them and burned them in public. After months of court hearings into Saris's affairs, the final verdict was delivered. They forgave him on the grounds that he had paid some of his own expenses in Japan on behalf of the company, and for his merits in obtaining favourable terms of trade in Japan. They also paid him a large sum of money as compensation for the confiscation of the goods he had obtained through private trade. Saris later married Anne, daughter of William Meggs of Whitechapel, and lived a quiet life until his death in 1643.

6

Waning Influence

I could not even speak to the officials, let alone the emperor.
Everything has changed so much.
Letter from WILLIAM ADAMS to Jacques Specx, 14 October 1616

In his later years, Adams struggled to keep up with the great
changes taking place in Japan's political landscape. His despair
is evident in the letters he wrote at the time. In the absence of his
former influence, Adams had to rely on his patience to overcome
the difficulties that stood in his way.

Selling Cannon to the Shogun

After Saris left Hirado, Cocks set up branches in various parts of
Japan to sell English goods. He sent William Eaton to Osaka and
Richard Wickham to Sunpu and Edo. They were hosted in the
houses of local merchants, and bought and sold goods with their
help. While in Edo, Wickham stayed with Adams.

Adams travelled back and forth between Hirado and the various branches, handling the delivery of letters and money. He also
acted as an intermediary, advising on business with local merchants in various places. In addition to Adams, his servants often
provided services to the English trading post. Cocks's letters show
that Adams performed his duties well, but his relations with his
fellow countrymen were sometimes less than harmonious.

In particular, the relationship between Adams and Wickham did not flourish. In a letter dated January 1614, Cocks advised Wickham to be kind to Adams and not to quarrel with him. As was clear from his discussions with the Jesuits, Adams never backed down once an argument had begun. But Wickham didn't trust Adams. On one occasion, Cocks followed Adams's advice and sent a large quantity of woollen cloth to Edo by ship; however, it took three months to get there owing to adverse winds and accidents. The Dutch transported their woollen cloth overland and arrived in Edo over two months earlier. By the time the English cloth reached Edo, the market was already saturated, and demand was at its lowest ebb. In a letter dated 22 May 1614, Wickham blamed Adams for giving such damaging advice. Merchants trading in Nagasaki told him that they never brought goods from there by sea, since the overland route was faster and safer. He even suspected Adams of secretly working for the Dutch. However, these allegations were unfounded.

Despite these strained relations, Ieyasu purchased a large quantity of cloth and lead from the English, thanks to Adams's mediation. Lead was used to make bullets and cannonballs. Because there was a shortage in Japan, the Japanese relied on imports. Ieyasu also considered purchasing cannon and gunpowder. Before coming to Japan, Saris took four culverins and two sakers out of the other two ships in his fleet to bring them to Japan on the *Clove*. A culverin was a fairly large cannon, while a saker was a slightly smaller cannon, mostly used on ships. Saris brought these cannons because he had heard from a Dutchman that they were in demand in Japan. Cocks sent Adams to Sunpu to sell the cannon to Ieyasu, who ordered them to be delivered to Edo. As the cannons were heavy to transport by land, Adams probably argued that they should be sent by sea along with the cloth. Ieyasu bought the four culverins and one saker. The other saker had previously been sold to the lord of Hirado.

Around the same time, Ieyasu also bought cannon and lead from the Dutch through Lodensteijn. There had been no war in Japan for thirteen years since the Battle of Sekigahara, so why would Ieyasu be so keen on buying ordnance and ammunition at this time? While there was peace, Japan was divided into two seats of power. The shogun was the actual ruler of Japan, especially in the eastern part of the country. While his son Hidetada took over the title of shogun from his father in 1605, the real power remained in Ieyasu's hands. He became *ōgosho*, meaning 'retired important person', in this case 'retired shogun'. In this role, he presided over all decisions, with Hidetada complying with what Ieyasu advised.

The area west of Kyoto was being ruled by warlords loyal to the Toyotomi clan. Most of them were not under Ieyasu's control. They posed a threat to the power of the Tokugawa. When Hideyoshi's son Hideyori came of age, he was likely to be appointed kanpaku, as his father had been. The rank of kanpaku, or 'regent of the emperor', stood above the rank of shogun. This would mean that the Toyotomi would once again rule Japan. If the western warlords supported Hideyori, it could even lead to the total overthrow of the Tokugawa.

Ieyasu's political base was therefore weaker than it appeared to be. To counter these dangers, he built up his own power base in eastern Japan. The shogunate became the real political power, and Hideyori had power only in his own domains. By Hideyoshi's will, Hidetada's daughter Sen-hime was married to Hideyori. This brought the two clans closer together. However, Hideyori's mother Yodo-no-kata didn't trust Ieyasu, and she would not allow her son to leave Osaka Castle to meet him. The only time they met was in 1611, when Ieyasu stayed at Nijō Castle in Kyoto, near Osaka. At that time, Ieyasu invited Hideyori to visit him. At first, Yodo-no-kata refused; it was only after Katō Kiyomasa and Asano Yoshinaga, the two leading warlords of the western camp, promised to protect Hideyori during his visit that Yodo-no-kata allowed him to leave for Kyoto.

The meeting itself took place in a friendly manner. Ieyasu showed his utmost respect and Hideyori responded in kind. Legend has it that Ieyasu was impressed with Hideyori's strong presence. Some believe that this event raised in Ieyasu's mind the possibility that Hideyori might displace Hidetada from power after his own death. Ieyasu did not trust Hidetada's abilities, especially on the battlefield, and here at Nijō Castle stood a man who looked capable.

Soon after, several of Hideyori's greatest allies, including Kiyomasa and Yoshinaga, succumbed to illness. This weakened the Toyotomi clan to such an extent that the balance of power between the two clans moved completely to the Tokugawa. In such a sudden shift, war often becomes inevitable. Ieyasu's purchase of cannons and ammunition from the English and Dutch should be seen in this context: he was one who prepared for the worst, and since Hideyori lived in Osaka Castle, these weapons could be of use in the event of a siege.

At the same time, Ieyasu feared a Christian uprising. On 31 January 1614, he issued a decree banning Christianity through-out the country and exiling all priests and monks. He ordered the warlords to destroy all churches and to force Christians in their territories to renounce their faith. Despite these harsh measures, some priests continued their missionary work in hiding. According to Dutch and English sources of the time, there were disturbing rumours of mutiny and war. But Adams had other things on his mind. On 20 July he returned to Hirado, where he set about rigging a junk. Cocks intended to send Wickham on this junk to Siam to establish trade between Japan and Siam, and appointed Adams as captain of the ship. Adams looked forward to the voyage as it would give him an opportunity to use his navigational skills again.

Adams was also involved in the purchase of the junk. Lodensteijn had just returned from a voyage to Siam. Cocks wanted to buy Lodensteijn's junk because it was a sturdy ship capable of travelling long distances. But Adams objected, saying he did not trust Lodensteijn. Following this advice, Cocks invested his money in another junk, and Lodensteijn's ship was sold to the Dutch.

Troubles in Ryukyu

Cocks named the newly purchased junk the *Sea Adventure*, and placed great hopes in it for a profitable voyage to Siam. He gave Wickham a cargo of mostly cloth, Japanese weapons and armour, and some cash to the value of £1250, and instructed him to buy sappanwood, deerskins, raw silk and silk goods. Cocks included the Japanese armour because he had heard it was highly prized in Siam; he advised Wickham to use these as gifts for the king of Siam and other dignitaries. The only cause for concern was the discord between Adams and Wickham. In his instructions to Wickham, Cocks asked him not to offend Adams in any way. He urged him to be patient, for both his own sake and that of the Company.

In addition to Wickham as chief merchant and Adams as captain and pilot, the *Sea Adventure* also carried the merchant Edmund Sayers and Adams's friends Damian Marini, an Italian, and Juan de Lievana, a Spaniard. These two men were probably deserters from Vizcaíno's ship. Marini seems to have been an able pilot, and this may have brought him into close contact with Adams. In his journal of the voyage, Adams put the number of people on board the junk at between 120 and 130. This included the Japanese sailors and Japanese merchants who boarded as passengers.

As he was about to set sail, news reached Hirado that Ieyasu was approaching Osaka Castle with a large army. The precarious peace finally came crumbling down. Hideyori had been preparing for war through the gathering of rōnin, or masterless samurai. After the Battle of Sekigahara in 1600, the country was swarming with these rōnin. With no means of subsistence, they were only too happy to be hired by Hideyori. If they showed their diligence, they might be able to remain in his service and regain their pride. Ieyasu watched this development with unease.

Shortly afterwards, the Hōkōji bell incident occurred. The reconstruction of the Great Buddha Hall of Hōkōji Temple, ordered by Hideyori in accordance with Hideyoshi's dying wish, was completed in 1614. To celebrate, Hideyori had a large bell made, and a monk named Seikan came up with an inscription for the bell: 'Kokka Ankō, Kunshin Hōraku', which meant something like 'May the state be at peace and secure. May the lord and his vassals be rich and merry.' As such, the text was idiomatic, but there was a problem with the kanji used in these inscriptions. The kanji for both Ieyasu's and Toyotomi's names were used. While the two kanji for Ieyasu were separated from each other, those for Toyotomi were together. This was interpreted as a curse on Ieyasu and a desire for the Toyotomi clan to prosper. It was also unheard of to use the kanji of the first name 'Ieyasu', and these aspects were seen as a mockery of him. This infuriated Ieyasu and gave him a pretext to wage war against Hideyori.

Ieyasu ordered all the warlords in the country to go into battle. He besieged Osaka Castle with an army of over 150,000 men (the Winter Campaign). By this time, Ieyasu's power was so well established that no warlord dared to side with the Toyotomi. Hideyori had only a small army of direct vassals, but he had hired a large number of rōnin, some of whom proved to be fierce warriors. Before he left for Siam, Adams heard that fighting had already begun. Praying for Ieyasu's victory and hoping for a smooth voyage, Adams raised the anchor of the *Sea Adventure* and set sail from Hirado on 28 November 1614.

The *Sea Adventure's* voyage was beset by a series of misfortunes from the outset. Shortly after setting sail, headwinds prevented the ship from sailing and forced the English to anchor in Kawachi Bay, a short distance south of Hirado. While waiting for a favourable wind, they discovered that the *Sea Adventure* had several leaks. Adams instructed his sailors to plug the leaks and thought the problem was solved. After three weeks of waiting, the wind shifted, and Adams gave the order to set sail. Having passed south of the Gotō Islands, Adams changed course to the southwest, but by this time the ship was leaking water again in several places, and the sailors were busy day and night pumping out the seawater. On 19 December, they were caught in a storm, which exacerbated the leaks. The crew were exhausted from the constant pumping out of seawater; only fifteen of them could stand on their feet, and the rest were either seasick or half-dead from the labour.

The merchants were terrified at the sight of the leaks. They were in uproar, saying that the English had taken them out in a rotten junk to drown them. Together with the sailors, they urged a change of course from China to the Ryukyu Islands. This archipelago lay to the south of Japan. The warlord Shimazu of the Satsuma domain in southwest Kyushu had conquered the islands in 1609, but the actual government was still in the hands of Shō Nei, the native king who resided on the main island of Okinawa. At first Adams refused, believing they were close enough to the Chinese coast to make it, but the sailors threatened to stop pumping. Realizing the gravity of the situation, Adams relented and changed course for Ryukyu, entering a bay northwest of Amami Ōshima, a large island also under the rule of Shō Nei between Okinawa and Kyushu, at midnight on 22 December.

Anchored in the bay, the sailors searched for the leaks and set about repairing them. A short time later, the island's governor came aboard with a large contingent. He promised the English friendship, but advised them to move to Naha, the main port of the Ryukyu Islands. So Adams set sail for Naha and arrived safely on 27 December. The next day they received permission from King Shō Nei, who lived in the royal town of Shuri, to unload their cargo. When all the goods were unloaded, they brought the junk ashore. But when they tried to repair the leaks, the sailors wouldn't cooperate. This meant that the officers had to carry out the repairs alone. The locals were also reluctant to supply the necessary materials.

To solve the problem, Adams entrusted two messengers with a letter and sent them to Shuri. A week later, on 15 January, the Ryukyu king's representative arrived in Naha and arranged for the necessary materials to be sent. Much time had been lost, and Adams was worried about the direction of the seasonal winds: if they left too late, they would not be able to reach Siam. By 25 January, the ship's repairs were almost complete. The next day, Adams rushed to get the ship ready to sail. But then a serious problem arose: frustrated at being stranded in Naha, the sailors demanded that Adams pay them their wages in advance. Adams refused, since their contract stipulated that half their wages would be paid on arrival in Siam and the other half on their return to Hirado.

Then the merchants came to him to plead for the sailors. They asked Adams to give them at least some of their wages, since the voyage was taking longer than they had planned, but Adams, feeling that he could not disobey the rules of the Company, firmly refused. He spent the next day discussing the matter with the merchants and Wickham. It was the boatswain and a few mutineers who instigated the dispute over wages. Wickham was furious and insisted that he would never sail with them, so it was decided to remove the mutineers from the ship.

This, however, did not solve the problem. The other sailors said they would not go on board unless they were paid half their wages in advance. Unable to sail without them, Adams finally agreed.

Now he was ready for the voyage, but things didn't go as Adams had planned. Yet, in the midst of this tense situation, some good news found him. A warlord who had fled the fighting in Osaka reached Naha, and told Adams that Ieyasu had won the battle. Adams was delighted to hear this.

On 11 February, the ship was ready to sail. But the sailors did not come on board because Adams had asked them to submit a receipt for the advance payment of half their wages. After much ado, the case was settled with Adams paying them without a receipt. By the time the sailors finally boarded the ship, it was too late to depart. Over the next few days, storms raged and sailing became impossible. By now, the time to take advantage of the seasonal winds had passed. On 16 February, Adams convened a committee of officers to discuss what to do; they decided to stay in the Ryukyus and return to Japan in October.

Two days later, Adams received a visit from the king's secretary. He was told not to fit out his ship at Naha and to leave within three months. Adams's journal doesn't mention what he said in response; he must have been at a loss. His only comment is: 'So this day ended. It rained very much.' The English did not seem to be leaving soon. The governor of Naha was concerned about this and visited Adams at his lodgings on 19 February. He asked him if he would return to Japan or wait for the seasonal winds in spring. Adams replied that he didn't know – he had sent a letter to Cocks in Hirado on a Satsuma ship but had not yet received a reply.

On 21 February, he was visited by an envoy from Shuri. They demanded that Adams move to Amami Ōshima because a ship from China was due to arrive in three months' time. If the Chinese knew that Adams's junk was docked there, they might not come to Naha again. The lives of the people of the Ryukyus depended on trade with this one Chinese ship, which arrived every year around May. But Adams, who knew the dangers of sailing in such conditions, could not agree to this request. He replied that he did not care where he died, either here or at sea. But he prayed for mercy for the passengers and crew. With this answer he left them.

The envoy gave up trying to persuade him. All that remained for Adams was to wait for an opportunity to return to Hirado; there was nothing more he could do. Over the next few days, there was heavy rain and a northerly wind. Every day Adams walked about in a gloomy mood, checking the direction of the wind. Everyone was losing patience with the situation: Adams's friend Marini clashed with Wickham, and the morale of the crew sank. On 5 March, the officers, sailors and merchants rose up in arms to fight each other. Adams, Wickham and Sayers intervened to separate the two sides. After much persuasion, the fighting came to an end, fortunately with no bloodshed.

At this point, Shōbei, a merchant and friend of Adams, approached the market with sixteen or twenty men armed with pikes, *naginata* (a type of halberd) and bows and arrows to subdue the sailors. Adams, wishing to avoid the worst, kept his cool and persuaded the forty or so sailors to stay back. But the dispute between the sailors and the merchants did not end there. Adams had to spend his days trying to mediate between the two sides. He could no longer afford to worry about sailing the ship.

Meanwhile, the authorities at Shuri had become aware of the clashes. Finally, on 15 March, the warden of Shuri Castle arrived with his soldiers. In the presence of these soldiers, the parties to the dispute calmed down and agreed to stop fighting. Adams thanked the town officials for informing Shuri of the situation. With that settled, a relieved Adams was in high spirits, and his thoughts turned back to the preparations for sailing. Should they outfit the ship here or return to the Gotō Islands, an archipelago near Hirado? He discussed the matter with his officers but could not come to a definite answer.

Returning to the bitter reality of his situation, Adams became depressed again. On 24 March he received an invitation from

Shō Nei: the king wanted Adams to see the city of Shuri and attend a banquet. But Adams was not interested in such a leisurely entertainment under the circumstances. 'If I could not find that favour to trim our ship here, the sight of the city was no pleasure to me,' he replied.

In the meantime, Marini and Wickham had made peace. Easter fell on 26 March, and Adams and his friends spent the day in good spirits. But the ringleader of the sailors' rebellion started another riot, and that night, Shōbei killed him. Two days later, Shōbei attended the banquet in Shuri, where he was entertained by Shō Nei, and returned to Naha that evening. The death of the ringleader seemed to solve the problem, but disputes with the sailors continued. Two sailors were arrested by the local authorities for misbehaviour. Adams tried to get them released, but they were taken to Shuri to be tried under Ryukyuan law. The ship's officers arrested another sailor for theft. They wanted to cut him to pieces, but since they needed as many sailors as possible for the voyage back to Japan, Adams refused to let them and released him. Similar incidents continued, and Adams had his hands full dealing with them.

On 21 April, Adams thought about sailing for Japan, but the sailors again refused to come on board. Many of them had spent their wages, and some had no money left to pay their merchant hosts. They asked Adams to lend them some money, but Adams replied that he had not brought enough money with him to cover their expenses. If he did not pay them, however, he would not be able to set sail. Adams made the best of the situation and seems to have come to an agreement, but all this trouble delayed the departure once more.

In these circumstances, Adams's emotions ran high. His arguments with Wickham became more frequent, and on 7 May, they got into a big fight. Wickham accused him of not doing his best for the Company, and said that Adams was allowing Marini to trade privately. When Marini was called as a witness, Adams denied it. With no response from Wickham, the dispute ended without further discussion. Unknown to Adams, Marini was in fact trading privately, and Wickham, who had accused him, was doing a great deal of private trading himself. Both of these details would not come to light until later.

As Adams prepared to sail once more, he received word that another war had broken out between Ieyasu and Hideyori (the Summer Campaign) and that Ieyasu was likely to lose. When Adams heard this news, his heart must have been filled with anxiety. On 21 May, the *Sea Adventure* left Naha. It dropped anchor near the Gotō islands, southwest of Hirado, on 27 May and in Kawachi Bay, near Hirado, on 10 June. Adams thanked God for his safe return.

International Conflicts

The day after the *Sea Adventure* arrived, Cocks went to meet them in Kawachi, and brought Adams some welcome news. He had received a letter a few days earlier from Matsura Takanobu, lord of Hirado, who had taken part in the siege of Osaka on the side of the Tokugawa. The letter said that Ieyasu had taken Osaka Castle and that Hideyori and Yodo-no-kata had committed *seppuku*. Two days after receiving the letter, a Franciscan named Apollonario came to Hirado. He was in the castle when it fell but managed to escape. He told Cocks that he had nothing with him but the clothes on his back – everything had happened all of a sudden. He marvelled that Hideyori's army of 120,000 men could be defeated so quickly. At the time of the siege of Osaka, there were two Franciscans, two Jesuits and an Augustinian in the castle. Apollonario asked Cocks to give him something to eat, for he had endured much hardship on his flight, and after he had eaten, he left. When Adams heard that the man to whom he owed his life, had won, he must have felt relieved.

The voyage to Siam was a disaster, but at least Adams and the others returned safely. Yet the English blamed Adams for the failure. 'If Adams had not been Jan Joosten's enemy, he would have bought Jan Joosten's junk. With this junk he would have made the voyage unharmed and would not have been plagued by leaks,' wrote one Dutch merchant, who had heard it from others, in a letter to Specx dated 13 July 1615.

Complaints against Adams were not limited to the failure of the voyage to Siam. Shortly after his return to Hirado, a quarrel broke out between Adams's host, Yasaemon, and Cocks's servant. When Cocks complained to Adams, Adams came to Yasaemon's defence, vouching for Yasaemon's integrity at the cost of his own 'life and soul'. This attitude did not go down well with the English. 'He still esteemed Yasaemon more than all our English nation,' Cocks wrote in his diary, adding: 'both I myself and all the rest of our nation do see that he is much more friend to the Dutch than to the Englishmen, which are his own countrymen.'

The arrival of an English ship brought Adams a brief respite from this unpleasant mood. The *Hosiander*, commanded by Ralph Coppindale, called at Kawachi Bay on 31 August 1615. Since it was customary in Japan to pay homage to Ieyasu on the arrival of a ship, it was decided that Coppindale, together with Adams, Wickham and Eaton, should go to Kyoto where Ieyasu was staying. Just as he was about to prepare for the journey, Adams received a letter from Ieyasu asking him to come to Kyoto at once. No reason was given, but Adams assumed Ieyasu wanted to enquire about the Ryukyu kingdom. Being summoned by Ieyasu must have been a comfort to Adams's self-esteem.

On the morning of 11 September, Adams left for Kyoto with Coppindale and his party. On arrival in Kyoto, however, he was told that Ieyasu had already left the city and was on his way back to Sunpu. To catch up with him, Adams left Coppindale behind and went on alone. He found Ieyasu in Sunpu, where he was told the reason for the summons. The *San Juan Bautista* that Date had sent to New Spain had returned and landed at Uraga. It was carrying a delegation from New Spain with a letter from King Philip III of Spain. The letter made no mention of trade, only a request to protect the priests. This was unacceptable to Ieyasu, who had banished them from his domains. Moreover, the head of the envoy, Diego de Santa Catalina, and the other members were Franciscan friars.

Ieyasu sent Adams to explain to the envoy his edict against the priests. After arranging Coppindale's audience with Ieyasu, Adams departed for Uraga, where he informed Catalina of the ban. The Spanish friars were still granted an audience with Ieyasu, but this ended up being a hopeless affair: they knelt before him, delivered the gifts and left without a word being spoken. Catalina remained a prisoner for some time, after which he was deported.

The Spanish envoy was not the only matter on which Ieyasu consulted Adams. A month earlier, a Dutch ship had arrived in Hirado with a Portuguese junk, the *Santo Antonio*, which it had captured near Meshima, an island in Japanese waters. Specx had sent a letter to Ieyasu explaining the reason for the capture and later went to Kyoto himself to justify the Dutch action. He argued that the Iberians had not respected the truce of 1609 and had carried out large-scale attacks against the Dutch in the Moluccas and elsewhere. In revenge, Prince Maurice ordered the servants of the Dutch East India Company to seize any Iberian ships they encountered at sea. Specx therefore asked Ieyasu to give the Dutch the *Santo Antonio* as a war prize. The Portuguese in Nagasaki demanded the return of the junk, claiming that the seizure was illegal because it took place in the waters around Japan.

The *Santo Antonio* incident led to the formation of two factions within the shogunate. One, led by Hasegawa Fujihiro, the governor of Nagasaki, sided with the Portuguese and demanded the return of the junk. The other faction, which defended the

Dutch, was led by the lord of Hirado, Matsura Takanobu, who pleaded for the junk to be kept. Emotions ran high, and the two men clashed. Before Adams arrived in Sunpu, Ieyasu had already given the junk to the Dutch as a war prize. Ieyasu asked Adams why there was such hatred between the Iberians and the Dutch. It made no sense to him that they should be waging war in Asia while there was a truce in Europe. Adams replied that it was true that they had recently become friends through the mediation of the king of England and other potentates. But the king of Spain, by virtue of his foothold in the Philippines and other parts of Asia, thought himself more entitled to those parts of the world than any other Christian ruler, and therefore intended to prevent by force all other nations from trading in those parts. To which Ieyasu replied that the Spanish had no grounds for such claims. Since this was a dispute between European nations, Ieyasu would not interfere, leaving it to their rulers to decide at home.

But these were not the only two international conflicts to take place on Japanese territory during this period. While Adams was in Sunpu, a letter arrived from Cocks informing him that the Portuguese had captured his friends Marini and de Lievana in Nagasaki. When the Portuguese learned that they were working for the English, they laid hands on them and locked them in the carrack anchored off Nagasaki. When Cocks found out, he wrote a letter to the captain of the carrack, demanding that they be released, since they were under the jurisdiction of the English, not the Portuguese. He also sent a letter to Hasegawa Gonroku, who was governor of Nagasaki along with Hasegawa Fujihiro, asking him to intervene. However, Cocks received a contemptuous letter from the captain and nothing but words from Gonroku.

As a last resort, Cocks wrote a letter to Adams asking him to report the matter to Ieyasu. In the meantime, the Portuguese sentenced the pair to death, and a priest heard their confessions. To justify the execution, they gave Gonroku the records of the trial, which proved that the two men had committed treason against their king; however, Gonroku halted the execution and awaited Ieyasu's decision. Informed that his friend's life was in danger, Adams ran to Ieyasu and obtained a letter ordering the release of the two men. The case was closed, again against the wishes of the Portuguese.

Coppindale's meeting with Ieyasu proved to be a great success. Whereas the Portuguese and the Spaniards had to wait for months, Coppindale was granted an audience within two days of his arrival in Sunpu. Ieyasu welcomed him in a kind way. Adams's influence on Ieyasu contributed greatly to this benign mood. After the audience, Adams was about to leave Sunpu, but Ieyasu asked him to stay in Japan and not to go on any more voyages in junks. If the stipend he had given him was not enough, he would give him more. However, Adams replied that he had a contract with the East India Company, and it would be a disgrace if he did not fulfil his promise. From this anecdote, recorded in Cocks's letter of 25 February 1616 to the East India Company in London, we can see how Ieyasu became more and more attached to Adams as the years went by, but Adams felt he had a duty to his English employer. The *Sea Adventure* was ready for another voyage to Siam. Adams also wanted to make up for his last failed excursion. Interestingly, Adams's contract would expire during this voyage. Despite subsequent attempts by Cocks to persuade him not to go to Siam and to stay with Ieyasu, Adams remained determined.

The English left for Hirado in mid-November. Eager to secure the speedy release of his friends Marini and de Lievana, Adams left his fellow countrymen behind and went ahead. He arrived in Hirado on the evening of 27 November. The next morning, he hurried to Nagasaki with two members of the English trading post. There he gave the letter from Ieyasu to Gonroku. The day before, Gonroku had already released Marini and de Lievana from the carrack, having been informed in advance that Adams was coming. De Lievana, who had been ill, remained in Nagasaki. Marini, meanwhile, went with Adams to Hirado.

Locked up in the carrack, sentenced to death and even having made his confession, Marini said that every day he thought he was going to die. After a month in this state, the captain of the ship suddenly released him, but before doing so, the captain tried to persuade him to go with him, 'promising him mountains'. Marini refused and returned to Hirado with Adams.

On his return, Adams began preparations for his voyage to Siam. The *Sea Adventure* left Hirado on 6 December 1615, with Adams accompanied by Edmund Sayers. Cocks had given Adams £600 to buy sappanwood and deerskin. The voyage went well and the *Sea Adventure* arrived in Bangkok on 11 January. The junk of Shōbei, who had been with them in Ryukyu, also anchored there. In addition to his own trade, Shōbei would carry Siamese goods to Japan for the English. From Bangkok, Adams and Sayers went up the Chao Phraya River to Ayutthaya, then the capital, and presented gifts to the king. With the help of Benjamin Farie, the head of the English trading post in Siam, Sayers was able to buy a large quantity of sappanwood and deerskins. This took several months. The quantity of goods available was so great that they had to hire another junk in addition to the *Sea Adventure* and Shōbei's junk to transport all the goods to Japan.

But here again, discord occurred between Adams and his fellow countrymen. Many of the Japanese crew loaded sappanwood for their private account. Farie estimated that private goods took up two-thirds of the junk. There was not even enough room to load the goods purchased by the English. This did not sit well with Farie. In the first place, private trade was forbidden to servants of the East India Company. He asked Adams to be truly informed how much sappanwood the sailors carried aboard, but Adams denied, saying that they were all true men and might carry what they pleased. Furious, Farie wrote to Cocks complaining that the Company was being abused in this matter.

This incident caused a rift between Adams and the English in Siam. Even the Dutch noticed the discord: Maarten Houtman, the head of the Dutch trading post in Ayutthaya, reported it in a letter to Specx, who had been reappointed head of the Dutch trading post in Hirado. Houtman wrote that the English had treated Adams badly and that Adams was unhappy with them. During his stay in Ayutthaya, Adams visited Houtman several times, and they became friends. The Dutchman had a good impression of Adams. He described him as 'a good, honest, pious man who tries to establish friendly relations with everyone'. He was also sorry that Adams had been treated so unfairly; Adams always tried to give the best advice, but the English blamed him for everything that went wrong. Houtman felt that this treatment was not in their best interests: in his eyes, Adams didn't want to work for the East India Company any longer. With relations with the English at their lowest ebb, Adams sailed from Bangkok on 6 June 1616 and returned to Kawachi Bay, near Hirado, on 21 July. The next day, Cocks met him and told him that Ieyasu had died.

Hidetada's Edict

Somewhat distracting from this sad news was the arrival in Hirado of two English ships, the *Thomas* and the *Advice*, both of which arrived about ten days before Adams's return. Cocks was already preparing for the court journey to the shogun in Edo, now with no need to stop at Sunpu on the way. He left on 30 July, and Adams went with him, as well as a few other Englishmen, a Japanese interpreter and several servants. The party travelled by boat through the Seto Inland Sea and arrived in Osaka on 5 August. There they sent their luggage by small boat up the Yodo River to Fushimi.

The English rode on horseback via Fushimi to Edo. When they reached Fujisawa near the Miura Peninsula on 26 August, two of Adams's servants from Hemi's estate came to meet them. They brought a present of ten loaves of white bread, a dish of boiled beef and two bottles of wine with them. While the party proceeded to Edo, Adams went ahead to make his house in Nihonbashi ready for Cocks and his men to stay. When the English arrived in Edo the next day, Adams was waiting for them and took them to the residence. He arranged for an audience with Hidetada through Honda Masazumi, who had moved to Edo after Ieyasu's death and now served the shogun.

While preparing gifts for the audience, Cocks experienced several earthquakes. At about three o'clock in the afternoon, the tremors became so severe that he thought the house was going to fall on his head. He ran out of the door, the timbers making such a cracking noise that it was frightening to hear. 'It began little by little, increased till the middle and in like sort, went away again,' Cocks wrote in his diary. The earthquakes continued in the following days, but Adams's house escaped damage, unlike Lodensteijn, who lost his storehouse.

The English carried the gifts to the castle on 1 September. In the inner palace they found many lords who had come to honour the new ruler of Japan. Cocks estimated that there were over 10,000 people in the castle that day. On entering the palace, Cocks studied the interior. He noted in his diary that all the rooms were gilded, on both the ceilings and the walls, except for some paintings of lions, tigers, panthers, eagles and other beasts and fowls, all very vividly drawn. All the floors of the rooms in the palace were covered with tatami mats edged with damask or gold cloth.

Only Cocks and the merchants Eaton and Wilson were allowed to see the shogun. Hidetada sat on tatami mats on a raised platform with his legs crossed, wearing a light blue robe. To his right, close to the platform, sat three or four men with shaved heads. Even Masazumi couldn't enter the room. Hidetada called out to Cocks once or twice to come in, but he refused. Afterwards he understood that this was the right thing to do, so simply stood at the entrance for a while and then left. Both when he entered and when he left, Hidetada bowed his head, and that was it.

After presenting their gifts to the shogun, Cocks now awaited the reissue of their trade privileges. However, this took a long time. The shogun's councillors sent for Cocks more than twenty times to ask if the English were Christians. He replied that they were, but not like the Jesuits or Franciscans, who had been banished from England before he was born. In the end, they warned him that the English should not communicate with the priests, or they would consider them all as one sect. Hidetada took an even more hostile attitude to them than Ieyasu had done. The presence of priests and friars in Osaka Castle at the time of the siege seems to have contributed to this: Cocks wrote in his diary that on several occasions he was told by the Japanese that the priests were inciting their subjects to revolt against their rulers, and noted the extreme hatred they had for the priests.

Hidetada wanted to wipe out Christianity in Japan. While Adams waited in Edo Castle for the privileges to be renewed, Hidetada issued a new edict of prohibition on 8 September. This edict was much harsher than Ieyasu's, stating that if a priest was found in a house, everyone in the house and their relatives would be killed. But Hidetada's antipathy was not limited to the Spanish and Portuguese. He also seems to have distrusted the English and the Dutch, and unlike his father Ieyasu, he had no particular affinity for Adams.

Every day, Adams went to the castle to solicit for the privileges. To make matters worse, some bad rumours circulated about his person. The day after the edict was issued, Hidetada's secretary, Doi Toshikatsu, told Adams it had been reported that there were priests in his house in Uraga. Although the priests were Adams's sworn enemies, his Japanese wife was Catholic, and just five days earlier, Cocks had received a letter from her informing him that she could not go to Edo because of Spanish guests. These guests may have been merchants rather than priests, but Adams, sensing the danger, wrote to his wife to make sure no priests entered the house. The rumour persisted, however, and two days later he wrote again to emphasize that the edict must be obeyed to the letter, or they would lose their lives.

Having dispelled the rumours, Adams continued to go to the castle day after day. Each time he was told to come back the next day. In the past, he had access to Ieyasu at all times, but with Hidetada it was different. He had no choice but to endure. Three weeks later, on 23 September, the privileges were finally granted. Adams was relieved, but the delay was a stark reminder that he could no longer hope to enjoy the same influence as before.

Now that Adams and Cocks had permission to leave, their spirits lifted a little, and they decided to go to Hemi and Uraga to look at Adams's estates. They left Edo at ten o'clock in the morning of 26 September and arrived at Hemi about two hours before nightfall. Cocks explained in his diary that Hemi was a lordship given to Adams by the old shogun, and that his son Joseph would inherit it. The estate comprised over a hundred farms and households, all of which were his vassals. Adams had the power of life and death over them, like any other warlord. Several of his tenants brought Cocks gifts of oranges, figs, pears, chestnuts and grapes, of which there was an abundance in the area. They spent the night at Hemi.

The next morning, Adams led Cocks and his men to his house at Uraga in the pouring rain. They proceeded on horseback. The chief of the town accompanied them, along with many servants. These servants ran ahead of them, forming a small procession. When they arrived in Uraga, most of the neighbours came to visit them, bringing fruit and fish, and rejoicing to see Adams back. On

28 September, the party went by boat to a town called Misaki to visit the residence of Mukai Masatsuna. This old admiral of Ieyasu's naval fleet had assisted Adams in the construction of the Western-style sailing ships. Although not mentioned in Adams's letters, Cocks's diary and letters suggest a close relationship between Adams and Masatsuna, as well as his son Tadakatsu. Masatsuna kindly entertained the English at dinner and gave Cocks a *wakizashi* (short sword). Afterwards, his men showed the English his son's newly built house nearby, which made a good impression on Cocks.

The group spent the night at an inn in Misaki. Their host's eldest daughter was married to a Dutchman, probably a survivor of the *Liefde*'s crew. The next morning, they returned to Uraga by boat. To thank them for their hospitality, Cocks presented Adams's wife and children, Joseph and Susanna, with some gifts. In the relentless rain, the warmth of their hospitality created a cordial atmosphere among the English.

Towards the evening, a courier arrived from Osaka with a letter from Wickham, dated 19 September 1616. The letter said that an edict had been issued in Kyoto, Osaka and Sakai forbidding the Japanese to buy goods from foreigners. It also stated that all foreigners must leave for Nagasaki or Hirado; from then on, these would be the only places they were allowed to sell their goods. This news came as a bolt from the blue to Adams. Sensing the seriousness of the situation, Cocks promptly sent the English merchants who had accompanied him to Hirado and returned to Edo with Adams and Eaton.

This sudden change seemed strange to Cocks. They had been told in Edo that they would receive the same privileges as those granted by Ieyasu, so the circumstances did not add up. Neither Adams nor the Japanese interpreter he had brought with him could read the text, which was written in kanji (Chinese characters). When they finally found a monk with some knowledge of kanji, they were told that their trade was restricted to Hirado; all other places were forbidden. This was a significant change from Ieyasu's privileges, which allowed them to trade anywhere in Japan. It seems that Hidetada was playing a cheap trick when he assured the English that their position would remain the same. The Gokinai region, including Kyoto, Osaka and Sakai, was the commercial centre of Japan at that time, and home to all the wealthy merchants. In contrast, Hirado was only a small town; no local merchant could afford to buy the expensive English goods. Cocks therefore felt that if trade was restricted to Hirado, it could not continue, and the English trading post would have to be closed. Fearing the worst, he was determined to regain the former privileges at any cost.

On arrival in Edo, Adams visited Hidetada's secretaries Doi Toshikatsu and Honda Masazumi. He even went to the governor of Kyoto, Itakura Katsushige, who happened to be in Edo too. But each of them confirmed that everything had changed since Ieyasu's death and that they could do nothing to help. Masazumi, an old friend, told Adams that he himself no longer exerted the same influence as he did under Ieyasu. In Masazumi's opinion, it would be a loss of face for the shogun to revoke his edict so soon after he had issued it. He thought it better to comply for now and try again next year.

By this time, Adams had already been lobbying the officials of the shogunate for a fortnight. Cocks gave up hope of regaining the former privileges and drew up a petition to be allowed to sell only his remaining goods in Kyoto. Adams had to wait until 15 October for Hidetada's final reply. In the end, the shogun granted no changes to the privileges, but for the time being the goods in Kyoto could be placed in the custody of a Japanese merchant to make sales for the English. After consulting with Eaton, Cocks decided it would be better to leave the goods in Edo with Adams, who could sell them in their absence. Adams was not subject to the restrictions imposed on foreigners because of his status as *hatamoto*.

The sudden changes shocked Adams, and we can see his bewilderment in a letter he wrote to Jacques Specx on 14 October 1616. In the letter he recounted the futility of his efforts to regain the privileges. He complained that he could not even speak to the officials, let alone the shogun. 'Everything has changed so much,' he exclaimed. In his opinion, the priests were to blame for the situation.

Hidetada's dislike of Catholic priests led him to issue an anti-Christian edict even more severe than Ieyasu's. It is ironic that the English and Dutch, who had warned the shogunate of the danger of a Spanish invasion, were also targeted. In a letter dated 14 January 1617 to Sir Thomas Smythe, governor of the East India Company, Adams explained that the policy was to prevent priests from entering the country as merchants. This seems close to the truth when compared with the contents of Cocks's diary, which records the same story. However, in a broader perspective, this should be seen as a first step towards complete control by the shogunate over all foreigners and foreign trade.

At nine o'clock in the morning of 17 October, Adams and Cocks set out on horseback from Edo. They spent the night in Kanagawa, where they met the Dutch envoy to Edo and exchanged information about the situation. The next day the English visited the old town of Kamakura. Three days later, they crossed the Hakone Pass, and on 21 October they had lunch at Kanbara.

As they passed through Yui, a bird suddenly flew out of a hedge, causing Adams's horse to start; Adams fell backwards and dislocated his right shoulder, and nearly broke his neck. Cocks rushed him to a nearby house and called for a bone setter. The shock of the political upheaval must have so upset Adams that he became careless and prone to accidents, as is often the case in such circumstances. Adams, feeling better, reached Sunpu with Cocks

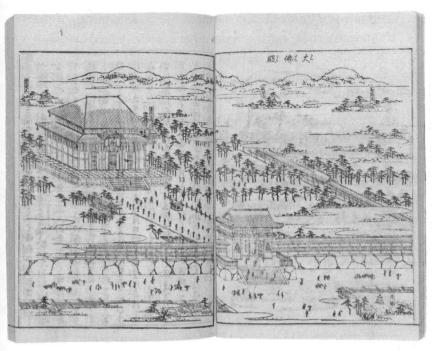

Hōkōji Temple, illustration from *Miyako meisho zue* (1786).

the next day, but his shoulder became so painful that he feared it might have dislocated again, and he decided to rest at Sunpu for four or five days. Cocks and Eaton hurried on and arrived in Kyoto a few days later, where they found Wickham.

While waiting for Adams, Cocks visited Hōkōji Temple. This was the site of the infamous bell that caused the siege of Osaka. Cocks marvelled at the huge bronze statue of Buddha, whose head reached to the top of the temple, although he was sitting cross-legged. The statue was covered in gold, and the temple itself was the tallest building that Cocks had ever seen. (Sadly, it was later destroyed by fire.) Cocks also visited other temples, such as the Sanjūsangendō Temple, which had a large wooden Buddha statue and 999 (Cocks wrote 3,333 in his diary) other brass statues on either side. He also visited the Toyokuni Shrine, where he saw the sculpture of Hideyoshi and admired the craftsmanship of the building, which far surpassed the others. Adams joined Cocks on 2 November, still with pain in his shoulder. On 11 November, having completed their business in Kyoto, the party left the city for Osaka and Sakai to complete the rest of their business and to say goodbye to the local merchants. Finally, on 25 November, they left Osaka by ship for Hirado, arriving there at sunrise on 3 December.

Troubles at Hirado

Relations between Adams and the English at Hirado remained tense. The Japanese scrivano (purser) on board the junk, hired by the English in Siam, was suspected of keeping some of the company's cargo for himself. Adams was furious and took on all the English in his defence. This reaction appalled Cocks, who had made every effort to maintain friendly relations with him. 'I take God to witness I do what I can to keep in with this man,' he wrote in his diary. Shortly after the incident, however, they reconciled, and Adams invited all the English to a banquet with a kabuki performance. Kabuki was not the classical, stylized Japanese theatre performed only by men, as we know today. In those days, kabuki meant girls dancing to music and songs. Eventually, by decision of the lord of Hirado, the scrivano's cargo became the property of the East India Company.

On 23 December 1616, Adams ended his employment with the company. Three years and one month after the contract was signed, Adams received his wages and was free to go. Meanwhile, Cocks wanted to sell the junk he had hired in Siam. When Adams left Ayutthaya as captain of the *Sea Adventure*, there was not enough room in his and Shōbei's junk to load all the goods. So they hired another junk with a crew, with Nochoda Liqwan as captain. Sayers boarded it to look after the company's goods. The three junks sailed from Siam to Japan but became separated during the voyage. Adams's junk arrived safely at Hirado, and Shōbei's at Nagasaki, but Sayers's junk did not reach Kagoshima until 20 September, after more than three months at sea.

Many of the crew, including the Chinese captain, lost their lives due to illness, and Sayers had to take on 38 new crew members in Satsuma to get the junk to Hirado. The junk barely made it. On arrival it became the property of the East India Company in exchange for the dead captain's debts, but the hull was so badly damaged that Cocks was unable to find a buyer. Adams proposed to buy it for the bargain price of 7,000 taels (Japanese silver ingots). He named the junk the *Gift of God*, the name of a ship that took part in the battle against the Spanish fleet in 1588.

After consulting with Cocks, Adams decided to use this junk to travel to Cochin-China (Quang Nam, in what is now central Vietnam). The area was ruled by the Quang Nam Nguyen clan. Their capital, Faifo (Hoi An), at the mouth of the Thu Bôn River, had become an international trading centre with many Chinese junks calling at the port in the early seventeenth century. Cocks had sent Tempest Peacock and Walter Carwarden there two years earlier in 1614, but Peacock was murdered and Carwarden disappeared. The company's money and the goods they were carrying were stolen. Having obtained from Hidetada a red seal pass for Cochin-China, Cocks asked Adams to go there. He rented space in Adams's junk for Sayers to accompany him and establish trade relations there. Cocks also asked them to make enquiries about the incident and demand the return of the stolen money.

Adams spent the next few months preparing his junk. When a wooden ship made an ocean voyage, it needed extensive repairs before it could sail again. During the preparations, he incurred the wrath of the lord of Hirado, Takanobu. Unable to obtain the quality timber needed to repair the ship in Hirado, Adams bought some in Nagasaki. This displeased the lord, and he sent Adams a letter condemning him for not buying timber from Hirado. He even forbade him from using Hirado carpenters. Adams did not take this well; he replied that since he had the red seal pass of the shogun, he would do as he pleased. This dispute seems to have been settled quickly, however. A few weeks later, Takanobu wrote a letter to the king of Quang Nam in which he recommended Adams to him.

But that was only the beginning of Adams's troubles. Next came a dispute with his host, Yasaemon. The aforementioned scrivano, who had attempted to embezzle the company's cargo, made a claim for damages against Yasaemon, who had given the scrivano's alleged share to Cocks. Just before Adams sailed for Cochin-China, Yasaemon sent one of his servants aboard the junk, hoping that Adams would come to his defence. However, Adams was ready to sail, so he told him to go to Cocks, who was in charge.

That very afternoon, the *Gift of God* set out to sea for Cochin-China. Shortly after setting sail, a small boat approached. Its crew asked him to stop, which he did, dropping the anchor. From the boat, several of Yasaemon's relatives climbed onto Adams's junk and grabbed his arms; before he knew it, they had gripped him so tightly that he was in great pain. Another grabbed the chest of John Pheby, his Japanese boatswain. One of Yasaemon's followers pulled his arm from his *kosode*'s sleeve as if to cut him with a knife; another one put his hand on the hinder part of Sayer's hair, all in as violent a manner as could be. This moved Adams to take out the red seal pass, kiss it and hold it over his head. This was his way of protesting and bearing witness to the violence they had inflicted on him. Seeing this, the attackers fled into the boat and headed for the shore without saying a word.

After the incident, Adams was forced to return to Kawachi Bay owing to contrary winds, and from there he wrote to Cocks about what had happened. Cocks wrote back that he would bring the matter to the lord of Hirado, but Adams replied that he didn't want to make public the violence he had suffered. If such an act of violence reached the ears of the lord, the only option would be the death penalty. Adams was shocked, but it was still in his heart to protect others.

On 23 March 1617, with a fair wind, Adams set sail again. After a smooth voyage, the *Gift of God* arrived in Faifo on 20 April. The king's secretary welcomed them but didn't give them permission to appear before the king himself. When they enquired about the English merchants who had been murdered three years earlier, they were given conflicting answers. They learned that Peacock's bad behaviour had something to do with it, but the rest was shrouded in mystery. As the incident had taken place without the king's knowledge, nothing more could be done. Recovery of the money and goods was out of the question.

Faifo seems to have been an unsafe place. Both Adams's and Sayers's diaries contain frequent references to murder and theft during their stay there. They themselves were victims of theft, but fortunately were not involved in any other serious incidents. The king granted them free trade and for the next two months they devoted themselves to business.

Adams set sail on 1 July and returned to Hirado on 11 August, where he found the English ship the *Advice* anchored. There happened to be fifteen Japanese sailors on board who had sailed to England with Saris on the *Clove*. After spending three months in England, they went to Bantam on another English ship, and from there returned to Japan on the *Advice*.

These people annoyed Cocks very much. According to their contract, they were to receive three years' wages on their return. However, they demanded more than the agreed salary. When Cocks rejected their request, the sailors went to Adams's lodgings and asked him to defend their case. But when Adams refused to support their demands, one of them grabbed him by the throat. Mansho, the interpreter who came to Adams's aid, was severely beaten. Stubborn as he was, Adams wouldn't back down, and the sailors took their case to the lord of Hirado. Cocks presented the books of account and the receipts for the wages that had already been paid, and his claims were found to be correct. In the end, the lord's brother sent word that the sailors should be paid according to the face value of the contract, and the case was settled. Still, being attacked twice in Hirado in such a short time must have eaten away at Adams's confidence. His former prestige as Ieyasu's confidant was fading.

Patience

Upon his return from Cochin-China, Adams received a pleasant request from Cocks to accompany him on his court journey. At the time, Hidetada stayed in Kyoto, so Cocks headed in that direction. Apart from the annual obligation to present the gifts brought by the newly arrived ship, Cocks wanted to petition for the repeal of the decree restricting trading places. He also wanted to obtain red seal passes for voyages to Siam and Cochin-China.

On 26 August, the party left Hirado by ship. Adams travelled in his own bark (a small sailing vessel), but his journey did not go smoothly. On the way, he became separated from Cocks's ship, and on top of that, he discovered a leak in the hull, which caused severe water damage to the goods he was carrying from Cochin-China. The bark itself sank and Adams had to change to another, smaller ship at short notice. Because of all this, Adams arrived in Osaka four days later than Cocks. The next day, they went to Kyoto together. Hidetada was at Fushimi Castle and after consulting with the lord of Hirado in Kyoto, they also went to Fushimi, where they met the Dutch, who had just finished their audience.

In the same year, the Dutch attacked Manila and captured many ships sailing to and from the Spanish colony. The Spanish, Portuguese and Chinese demanded that Hidetada expel the

Dutch from Japan as pirates, but Hidetada replied that he would not take part in disputes outside Japanese territory. There was a glimmer of hope for Adams, since the accusations of piracy were limited to the Dutch and did not target the English. Adams visited Hidetada's secretaries, Doi Toshikatsu and Honda Masazumi, and asked for an audience. Shortly afterwards, they were able to appear before Hidetada. Cocks presented the gifts and gave the shogun a letter from King James in reply to Ieyasu's letter three years earlier.

On 17 September, Adams went to Fushimi Castle and presented a petition for the abolition of trade restrictions. The secretaries told him to return the next day as it was too late. From then on, Adams waited at the castle every day for an answer. As had been the case the previous year at Edo Castle, he was told every time to come back later. He went to the castle in the morning and waited until nightfall without eating, day after day. In the end, Adams's patience paid off. On the 23rd, a week after he had begun to commute, he received a reply from Hidetada, but it was not what the English had expected. Hidetada would give the English no more privileges than other foreigners had.

As in the previous year, the reason given was to prevent priests from entering the country disguised as traders. But this time Adams learned of another reason. It was Hidetada's wish that domestic sales should be made by Japanese, not foreigners, and that the profits should go to the Japanese. Until 1616, the Dutch and English had sold their goods directly in the major trading centres of Kyoto, Osaka and Sakai, and sometimes in Edo. After the edict, however, they had to sell their imported goods in Hirado. A select few wealthy merchants sent their agents to buy the goods there. These merchants then distributed the goods within the domestic market. In this way, the merchants could make huge profits, since they dominated the market. These merchants were close to the shogunate, which allowed the shogunate to control the trade. While Ieyasu wanted to stimulate the economy through free trade, Hidetada restricted free trade and concentrated the profits of trade in the hands of a few wealthy merchants. This led to more control but less economic vitality.

In these circumstances, it did not matter how many times the English asked for the restrictions to be lifted; the shogun would never listen. All Adams could do was try to get an answer to King James's letter and red seal passes to travel to Siam and Cochin-China. To this end, he went to the castle every day. After a week had passed, he received a surprising reply: Hidetada told him that he would not answer King James's letter because it was addressed to Ieyasu and not to him. Moreover, it would be an ominous thing to do, since Ieyasu was dead. He only granted the two red seal passes to the English.

Having done what they could in Fushimi, Cocks and Adams visited Kyoto, Sakai and Osaka before returning to Hirado. At Cocks's request, Adams stayed on in Osaka to collect debts and accounts owed to the East India Company by local merchants, but some were reluctant to pay. It was not until 22 December that Adams returned to Hirado with the money he had collected.

Caught between the Dutch and the English

When Cocks left for Hirado, Adams asked him to find a buyer for the *Gift of God*: his last trip to Cochin-China had ended in a loss, and he wanted to get rid of the junk. Cocks did his best and found a buyer while Adams collected the outstanding debt. The junk was sold to a Chinese merchant for 1,200 silver taels. Cocks informed Adams of this good news in a letter dated 26 November, and through Cocks's efforts, he made a handsome profit.

On his return to Hirado, Adams decided to board the *Advice* and return to England. However, when a Chinese merchant named Higo Shikan offered him the chance to pilot a junk to

Cochin-China, Adams's desire to return home vanished, and he accepted. Cocks rented part of the ship's hold. Sayers would go with the junk as merchant in charge.

The voyage was a disaster from the start. Shortly after setting sail from Nagasaki on 17 March 1618, the junk was caught in a storm and ran aground off the Gotō Islands, damaging the rudder. After a quick repair, they attempted to continue their journey, but the rudder was damaged again on the way, so the ship stopped at Amami Ōshima to have a replacement rudder made from scratch. They stayed on the island for twenty days, but since he couldn't get suitable materials, Adams was forced to return to Nagasaki. He arrived there on 7 May.

Two months later, on 20 July, he received a request from Specx to go to Edo with the Dutch envoy Jan Berckhout. When Adams was employed by the English, the Dutch used Lodensteijn instead of Adams. However, Lodensteijn had a tendency to speak false-hoods and fell out of favour with Hidetada and his secretaries. During the court journey the previous year, Lodensteijn told the Dutch to go directly to the castle without contacting the lord of Hirado. This broke protocol and caused embarrassment to the Dutch. Now that Adams was free, Specx was eager to have him back in service, and after consulting Cocks, Adams agreed. He left Hirado just before noon on 31 July, accompanying Berckhout and his party.

As he passed through Shimonoseki, Adams heard a strange rumour. Some Japanese told him that the Dutch had captured five English ships and taken one of them to Hirado. Adams said little, and divulged even less, but the Dutch heard about it too, as one of them spoke fluent Japanese.

Just before Adams arrived in Osaka, a courier sent from Hirado overtook him and delivered a letter written by Cocks. From its contents, Adams learned the details of the capture of an English ship by the Dutch. Adams likely knew that the competition between the Dutch and the English in Asia had intensified to the point of armed conflict. Still, the news must have been hard to swallow: if the English were his countrymen, the Dutch were also his friends. Cocks was on his way to Edo to lodge a complaint with the shogunate about the Dutch piracy. He wrote to Adams asking him to distance himself from the Dutch and wait for him. But Adams, who had a strong sense of duty, refused. Having given his word to accompany the Dutch to court, he could not afford to abandon the job, come what may. He wrote back to Cocks that he was no longer with the East India Company, and even tried to persuade Cocks not to go to Edo on the matter. When Cocks received this letter in Shimonoseki, he became furious. In his diary he cursed Adams's letter as unreasonable and lamented that Adams had become 'all together Hollandised'.

Why did Adams refuse Cocks's request? His sense of duty was partly a factor. But Adams was also well aware of the futility of appealing to the shogun. Many envoys had complained to Hidetada about Dutch piracy, but the shogun had always maintained a policy of neutrality. To dare bring the matter to Hidetada was to risk his wrath, which would put the English in an even worse position. But Cocks did not give up. He had been advised by a senior official of the lord of Hirado that he had a good chance of winning the case. So Cocks hurried to Edo. Meanwhile, Adams arrived in Edo with the Dutch envoy. Through Adams's mediation, the Dutch audience with Hidetada went off without a hitch. Satisfied, Berckhout and his party soon returned home.

While in Edo, Adams received a series of letters from Cocks and the other English merchants along the way. Having fulfilled his duty to the Dutch, Adams now decided to help them. Soon after the Dutch left Edo, Adams set off to meet Cocks. He joined Cocks in Kanagawa and accompanied him back to Edo. It was already 4 October 1618. Adams's children also came to greet Cocks and treated him to a banquet. In this convivial atmosphere, Cocks's resentment towards Adams for his perceived lack of cooperation quickly dissipated. The next day, they went to the residence of Takanobu, lord of Hirado. When they showed him the complaint they intended to present to Hidetada, Takanobu read it in silence. His retainer, Momono Tarōzaemon, also read it, with a troubled expression on his face. Like Adams, he tried to persuade Cocks not to press charges, but Cocks refused to listen.

Sensing Cocks's determination, Adams undertook the task of presenting the complaint to Hidetada, even though he knew it would be futile. This decision again shows that the English criticism of his lack of patriotism was unfounded. On 6 October, Adams first went to Edo Castle with Tarōzaemon to ask for an audience. Permission was soon granted. Three days later, Cocks and his party met Hidetada and presented him with the gifts, as was customary after the arrival of a new ship. The case against the Dutch, however, proved to be a much more difficult task. Adams went to the castle every morning and waited until night for an answer. Each time he was met with nothing more than a nod and a smile. (It didn't help that most of the officials had gone to pay their respects at the tomb of Ieyasu in Nikkō, a few days' journey from Edo.)

The other problem was the shogun himself. He refused to even take the time to listen to the English complaints. And Adams was not alone. Lodensteijn also waited there every day for the shogun. He wanted to present Hidetada with a gift and hoped to obtain a red seal pass to travel to Tonkin. Adams often saw Lodensteijn at Edo Castle, just standing there. Lodensteijn had lost much of his former vigour; he was heavily in debt and was treated coldly by the officials. But one day, Hidetada saw Lodensteijn standing in a corner with his gift. He asked his servants who this person was, and when they answered, he said, 'it is reported this fellow is much indebted and will not pay his creditors.' A friend of Lodensteijn replied that it was 'to the Hollanders, his countrymen and to no others'. His friend was lying, Cocks wrote, for he owed money to several other people. Nevertheless, having heard this, the shogun received Lodensteijn's gift and provided him with a red seal pass.

No such opportunity presented itself for Adams. A month and a half had passed since the audience when Cocks decided to return to Hirado. He left on 18 November. Adams remained in Edo and continued his daily visits, but he was unable to secure anything. The fact that Cocks had sold a red seal pass to another person the previous year was seen as a problem; if the matter was brought before the shogun, it would cost several men their lives, Cocks was told, so the new red seal pass he had applied for was hard to come by.

Eventually Adams also left Edo without the pass, having retained a servant. On 11 December, he joined Cocks in Osaka. There they waited for some time for the pass, but it still didn't come. After finishing their business, they returned to Hirado in a bark.

Adams's Last Will

The pass was finally handed over to them after their arrival in Hirado at the end of January 1619. Cocks consulted with Adams, who agreed to go to Tonkin as captain of a junk owned by Sagawa Nobutoshi, a senior member of the Matsura family. It is likely that the lord of Hirado was involved in the planning of this voyage. On 16 March 1619, Adams left Hirado for Tonkin, and after almost a month's voyage, he arrived safely at the mouth of the river. It so happened that Lodensteijn's junk was anchored there. Adams and Lodensteijn chatted for a while on board. Lodensteijn had come to Tonkin to trade, carrying the red seal pass that, as we have seen, he had gone to great lengths to obtain.

Tonkin was famous for its silk, and on arrival, the passengers on Adams's junk were busy buying the precious product. It took them three months to complete all the transactions. Adams bought silk goods on behalf of Cocks and several others, including Specx, with cash entrusted to him. After completing the purchases, Adams prepared to sail. At around midday on 16 July, the passengers boarded the junk, and at five o'clock in the afternoon, the anchors were hoisted and the ship set sail. They returned to Hirado about five weeks later, on 22 August.

By this time, Cocks had left for Kyoto to seek an audience with the shogun, who was back in the capital. On 21 September, the Dutch ship the *Engel* arrived in Hirado. Fighting between the two countries in Asia had intensified. As a result of one of these battles, the *Engel* brought several English prisoners of war to Hirado. When Adams heard of this, he went straight to Specx and persuaded him to release them.

Adams intended to follow Cocks to Kyoto, but fell ill and stayed in Hirado. When Cocks returned, he raised the idea of sending another junk. To equip the junk, Adams accompanied Cocks to Nagasaki on 16 February 1620. On his fourth day there, Adams became very ill again. He left Cocks in Nagasaki and hurried back to Hirado to see his physician and go to a hot spring for treatment, but neither seemed to help his recovery. Realizing that his death was imminent, on 16 May, he summoned Cocks, Eaton and several other members of the English trading post to his bed in the house of his host, Yasaemon. His condition was deteriorating, but his mind was still clear. In the presence of his fellow countrymen, Adams drew up a detailed will.

He divided all his money and possessions into two equal parts and bequeathed one half to his wife and children in England and the other half to his two children in Japan. To Cocks, he gave a celestial globe, all his maps and his best *katana*. He left the rest of his *katana* and *wakizashi* to his son Joseph. All his books and navigational equipment went to his friend Eaton. He also left money and goods to Yasaemon, several of his servants and various members of the English trading post. Adams had a concubine in Hirado with whom he had a child. It is not clear whether she received anything from Adams, but Cocks gave her some money to bring the child up.

At five o'clock in the afternoon on 16 May, the day on which his will was made, Adams departed this world. It was Cocks's and Eaton's responsibility to ensure that each person received Adams's belongings in accordance with his will. His son Joseph inherited his estate and became known as Miura Anjin. He was involved in the red seal trade until 1635, when a new edict was issued forbidding the Japanese from travelling abroad.

When Cocks visited Edo in December 1621, Joseph and Susanna met him at Shinagawa with a banquet, as before. The next day, Cocks delivered Adams's *katana* and *wakizashi* to Joseph. As he handed them over, Cocks's eyes filled with tears.

As Adams had predicted, the English trading post at Hirado failed to make a profit. Three years after Adams's death, on 23 December 1623, the post was closed, and Cocks left Japan with the rest of his staff. It was not until 231 years later that the English were allowed to trade in Japan again.

NOTES ON SOURCES

This book is based on primary sources. It is a non-fiction account of events as experienced by real people. In writing this book, I have used a large number of historical documents. Below, I give a brief overview of the main sources referred to in the text.

For information on Adams's career before he embarked on the *Liefde*, see the letter from Adams to his 'unknown friends and countrymen', 23 October 1611 (held in the India Office Records at the British Library, London) and a letter to his wife, circa 1611, published in Samuel Purchas, *Hakluytus posthumus; or, Purchas His pilgrimes* (London, 1625). Both letters are reproduced in volume I of Anthony Farrington's *The English Factory in Japan, 1613–1623*, 2 vols (London, 1991).

Information on the historical background to Queen Elizabeth's reign in England and on Adams's service as captain of a supply ship during the battle against the Spanish Armada in 1588 is given in William Murdin, *A collection of state papers relating to affairs in the reign of Queen Elizabeth* (London, 1759); and John Knox Laughton, *State papers relating to the defeat of the Spanish Armada, anno 1588* (London, 1894). On the Jesuit mission, see also Michael L. Carrafiello, 'English Catholicism and the Jesuit Mission of 1580–1581', *Historical Journal*, XXXVII/4 (December 1994), pp. 761–74. The story of the two Japanese boys on board Cavendish's ship is taken from Richard Hakluyt's *The Principal Navigations*, 3 vols (London, 1600), vol. III, p. 817.

For the voyage of the *Liefde*, in addition to the two letters by Adams mentioned above, I used the journal of Barent Jansz, a surgeon on board the *Geloof: Wijdtloopigh verhael* (Amsterdam, 1600). A reprint of Jansz's journal can be found in *De reis van Mahu en de Cordes* (The Hague, 1923), edited by the Dutch historian Frederik Caspar Wieder. This book also contains an extensive collection of documents relating to the Van der Haegen fleet. Records have survived of the interrogations of Dirk Gerritsz, captain of the *Blijde Boodschap*, and of his crew, who were captured by the Spanish in South America. These records, which contain a wealth of valuable information about the Van der Haegen fleet and Adams, are kept at the Archivo General de Indias in Seville. A reproduction of the original Spanish texts and a translation into Dutch can be found in J. W. IJzerman, *Dirck Gerritsz Pomp* (The Hague, 1915).

The events around the island of Santa Maria are described in detail in the above-mentioned letters by Adams and in a Spanish report by the viceroy of Peru (*Relacion muy circunstanciada de avisos de corsarios que tuvo el Virrey del Peru de la entrada que hiceiron en el Mar del Sur por el estrecho de Maggalanes en el año de 1599*), held at the Deposito hidrografico de Madrid. A reproduction and a Dutch translation of this manuscript can be found in the above *Dirck Gerritsz Pomp*. In addition to this valuable text, C. Errazuriz, *Seis años de la Historia de Chile* (Santiago de Chile, 1881) contains a study of the events in Chile from 23 December 1598 to 9 April 1605, based on primary sources, and reprints numerous extracts from these documents.

The events that occurred shortly after Adams's arrival in Japan are recorded in his letters. His conversations with Ieyasu in this book are taken entirely from the aforementioned two letters to his 'unknown friends and countrymen' and to his wife. The main Japanese sources relating to the arrival of the *Liefde* and Adams's activities are: *Ikoku nikki* (Tokyo, 1989); 'Tōdai ki', in *Zoku gunshoruijū* (Tokyo, 1995); 'Nagasaki kongen ki', in *Kaihyō sōsho* (Kyoto, 1928); 'Taihei zakki', in *Tsūkō ichiran* (Tokyo, 1940), vol. V, pp. 55–6.

For the cargo of the *Liefde*, I used the Jesuit historian Diogo do Couto's *Da Asia, Decada XII* (Lisbon, 1788). Couto's records are based on information transmitted to Portugal by the Jesuits. It is an invaluable source, but it cannot be relied upon in its entirety, as there are many inaccuracies. For example, according to Do Couto, the crew of the *Liefde* took part in the Battle of Sekigahara as gunners. The likelihood of this statement being accurate is extremely low. There is no mention of it in Adams's letters or in any of the Dutch sources. Moreover, all Japanese sources are silent on this subject. If Adams and his men had taken part in the battle, there would have been some mention of it in their letters or in Japanese sources. Do Couto's account is a secondary source, not based on actual observation, so if it is to be accepted as historical fact, it must be supported by primary sources that can stand up to historical criticism. For the cargo of the *Liefde*, however, Do Couto's list is supported by Dutch, Spanish and Japanese sources.

Do Couto also claims that Adams took part in the Dutch expeditions to the northeast in 1593, '94 and '95, but this is also doubtful since Adams makes no mention of this in any of his letters. This period coincides with Adams's employment with the Company of Barbary Merchants. As Adams was fond of talking about the Northeast and Northwest Passages, the Jesuits most likely misunderstood him to have been involved in these exploits.

For Jesuit accounts of Adams's arrival in Japan, see Fernão Guerreiro, *Relaçam annual das cousas que fizeram os padres da companhia de Iesus na India, & Iapão nos annos de 600 & 601* (Évora, 1603, original in the British Library); and Valentin Carvalho's letter of 8 February 1615, which can be found in Léon Pagès, *Histoire de la religion Chrétienne au Japon* (Paris, 1869, original manuscript preserved in the Academia de la Historia, Madrid).

We have two vivid accounts of the Franciscan 'miracle monger'. One is a letter from Richard Cocks to Thomas Wilson, dated 10 December 1614, now in the Public Record Office in London (reproduced in Farrington, *The English Factory in Japan, 1613–1623*). The other is by the Jesuit Pierre-François-Xavier de Charlevoix: *Histoire et description generale du Japon* (Paris, 1736). Charlevoix based his account on the letters of the Jesuits from Japan, which state that the incident took place in 1601. Adams's conversation with Pedro Morejón is recorded in a letter from the Jesuit Alessandro Valignano to the General Superior of the Jesuits, dated 20 October 1600. This letter is kept in the Jesuit archives in Rome. Louis Delplace gives a French translation in *Le catholicisme au Japon* (Brussels, 1909).

For Adams's debates with the Jesuits, I have used Francisco Pasio's *Lettres annales du Japon* (Lyon, 1609).

The information about the ships Adams built for Ieyasu is recorded in Adams's letter to his 'unknown friends and countrymen', and also in the *Keichō Kenmon-shū* (Tokyo, 1963). The details of Vivero's stay in Japan are recorded in the manuscripts *Relación que hace don Rodrigo de Vivero de lo que le sucedió volviendo de Gobernador y Capitán General de las Filipinas y arribada que tuvo en el Japón. Año de 1608* (copy in the Biblioteca Cervantina, Monterrey, Mexico); and *Relación y noticias de el Reino del Japón con otros avisos y proyectos para el buen gobierno de la monarquía española* (copy in the British Library). Reproductions can be found in Juan Gil, *Hidalgos y samurais: Espana y Japon en los siglos XVI y XVII* (Madrid, 1991).

Sources provide little information on Adams's Japanese wife, apart from some sporadic references in Richard Cocks's diary (preserved in the British Library), but there is an interesting account in W. Noel Sainsbury, ed., *Calendar of State Papers Colonial, East Indies, China and Japan*, vol. II: *1513–1616* (London, 1864), under the entry 'East Indies: December 1614', which describes his Japanese wife as a 'principal woman'. Jacques Specx's letter informing Adams of the arrival of a letter from his English wife, dated 25 August 1612, is preserved in the National Archives of the Netherlands in The Hague (1.04.02:1054). This bundle also contains other drafts of letters from Specx to Adams as well as Sprinckel's letters to Ieyasu and Adams. Gerard Reynst's letter to the 'Gentlemen XVII', or board of directors of the Dutch East India Company, about money sent to Adams's English wife, dated 26 October 1615, can be found in another bundle in the same archives (1.04.02:1058). These bundles belong to the archives of the East India Company (VOC 1.04.02). Together with those of the Dutch Factory in Japan (NFJ 1.04.21), both held at the National Archives of the Netherlands in The Hague, these archives contain many references to Adams, but have hitherto not been used much. For example, Houtman's letter about the troubles between Adams and the English in Ayutthaya, dated 8 June 1616, can be found in the archives of the Dutch Factory in Japan (1.04.21:276).

Puyck's journal of his court journey in 1609, and Specx's journal of his court journey in 1611, contain many references to Adams. Although both were servants of the East India Company, no copies of their journals survive in the archives of the East India Company. A copy of Puyck's journal is preserved in the Badische Landesbibliothek, Karlsruhe. Specx's journal was published by Isaac Commelin in *Begin ende Voortgangh van de Vereenighde Nederlantsche Geoctroyeerde Oost-Indische Compagnie* (Amsterdam, 1646).

Information about Dutch interference in Adams's correspondence can be found in a letter from Adams to Augustine Spalding dated 12 January 1613 (India Office Records, British Library) and in the journal of Peter Williamson Floris, a Dutch servant of the English East India Company, published in *Purchas his Pilgrimes* (London, 1625), part 3, p. 321.

The discord with Vizcaíno is described in the report of Vizcaíno's voyage to Japan, *Relación del viaje hecho para el descubrimiento de las islas llamadas ricas de oro y plata* (preserved in the Biblioteca Nacional de España in Madrid and reproduced in Juan Gil, *Hidalgos y samurais*), as well as in the aforementioned Specx's journal. References to Adams's advice to Ieyasu about a possible Spanish invasion can be found in *Relación de lo que sucedio a tres religiosos*, preserved in the Archivo General de Indias, Seville. A reproduction is included in *Dainihon shiryō* (Tokyo, 1968), vol. XII, no. 12. Other sources are the *Relación del P. Sebastián de San Pedro* and Valentin Carvalho's refutation of this *Relación*, kept in the Biblioteca nazionale centrale Vittorio Emanuele II in Rome.

A copy of John Saris's journal survives in the India Office Records at the British Library, and a reproduction can be found in Ernest M. Satow, *The Voyage of Captain John Saris to Japan, 1613* (London, 1900). Most of the documents relating to the English factory are contained in Farrington's *The English Factory in Japan, 1613–1623*. The work's two monumental volumes contain 437 reprints of historical documents, including eleven letters sent by Adams, four journals of Adams's travels, Adams's last will and testament, and letters and journals, accounts and diaries relating to the English Factory at Hirado. It is a treasure trove of information on Adams's activities since 1613. The diary of Richard Cocks is also a valuable source of information and is published by the Hakluyt Society as *Diary of Richard Cocks: Cape Merchant in the English Factory in Japan, 1615–1622* (London, 1883).

Suggestions for further reading:

Boxer, C. R., *The Christian Century in Japan, 1549–1650* (Berkeley, CA, 1951)

Corr, William, *Adams the Pilot* (Folkestone, 1995)

Irving, Richard, *A True and Complete Account of the Life of William Adams, the English Samurai* (2021–2)

Massarella, Derek, *A World Elsewhere: Europe's Encounter with Japan in the Sixteenth and Seventeenth Centuries* (New Haven, CT, 1990)

Rogers, P. G., *The First Englishman in Japan: The Life and Times of Captain William Adams, 1564–1620* (London, 1956)

Sadler, A. L., *Shogun: The Life of Shogun Tokugawa Ieyasu* (Rutland, 1978)

Screech, Timon, *The Shogun's Silver Telescope* (Oxford, 2020)

—, *Tokyo Before Tokyo* (London, 2020)

ACKNOWLEDGEMENTS

I am indebted to several archival institutions for their help. The Library of the International Research Center for Japanese Studies, in particular, has provided me with access to its archives and helped me to order books and reproductions. In addition, the National Archives of The Hague and the British Library have been of great assistance. The publication of this work was supported by the Great Britain Sasakawa Foundation. Part of the research in the Dutch archives for this book was funded by the Grant-in-Aid for Scientific Research on the Structure of Dutch–Japanese Relations in the Early Modern Period (JSPS Kakenhi 19K01010). Kataoka Mai, Ioka Utako and Ogawa Hitoshi helped me to gather all possible materials related to the study of Adams's life. I would like to take this opportunity to thank these people and many others who helped me in one way or another.

My friend and colleague Timon Screech encouraged me to publish this book. He spent a great deal of time reviewing the manuscript and pointing out countless interesting details. I am also indebted to another friend and long-time research partner, Cynthia Vialle, who directed me to the study of the archives of the Dutch East India Company. Through the many hours we spent together reading and analysing the Dutch sources, I was able to find much new and previously unknown information about Adams. She told me about the reference to Adams in Gerard Reynst's letter to the Heren Zeventien, which I might otherwise have missed. But to no one am I more indebted than to my wife, Keiko, who strongly encouraged me to write this book, reviewed the draft and gave me her full support in its preparation. To these three kind people, I express my deepest gratitude.

PHOTO ACKNOWLEDGEMENTS

The author and publishers wish to express their thanks to the sources listed below for illustrative material and/or permission to reproduce it. Some locations of artworks are also given below, in the interest of brevity:

From Isaac Commelin, ed., *Begin ende Voortgangh van de Vereenighde Nederlantsche Geoctroyeerde Oost-Indische Compagnie* (Amsterdam, 1646), photos courtesy of the International Research Center for Japanese Studies, Kyoto: pp. 50, 53, 59; from William Dalton, *Will Adams, the First Englishman in Japan: A Romantic Biography* (London, 1866), photo courtesy of the International Research Center for Japanese Studies, Kyoto: p. 37; maps courtesy of Futaka Kōhei: pp. 6, 7, 8; courtesy of Asano Miura: p. 139; Matsudaira Saifuku-ji Temple, Taitō: p. 120; courtesy of Nanban Bunkakan Museum, Osaka: pp. 117 (*bottom*), 119 (*bottom*); Nationaal Archief, The Hague: p. 170; National Archives of Japan, Tokyo: pp. 80, 81, 119 (*top*), 125; courtesy of National Museum of Japanese History, Sakura: pp. 114–15, 116 (*top*); courtesy of Osaka Castle Museum: pp. 113, 117 (*top*); Rijksmuseum, Amsterdam: pp. 25, 118; Shizuoka City Museum of Art: p. 116 (*bottom*); Smithsonian Libraries and Archives, Washington, DC: p. 201; from F. C. Wieder, *De reis van Mahu en de Cordes door de Straat van Magalhães naar Zuid-Amerika en Japan 1598–1600* (The Hague, 1923), photo courtesy of Harold B. Lee Library, Brigham Young University, Provo, UT: p. 39; Wikimedia Commons: pp. 27 (photo Ethan Doyle White, CC BY-SA 4.0), 140 (photo 江戸村のとくぞう, CC BY-SA 4.0).

INDEX

Page numbers in *italics* refer to illustrations